Praise for *The Vitruvian*

"I am a huge fan of Scott Grossberg and his wo.
*Vitruvian Square i*s one of the top five books on divination ever written. No matter what oracle route you wish to take, *The Vitruvian Square* will enhance your abilities and allow you to deliver distinct and specialized "readings" to anyone, at any time, and under any conditions. If that is not enough, *The Vitruvian Square* offers YOU a gateway to your own self-discovery and self-awareness, and spiritual practice. So, join us in *The Vitruvian Square*, won't you? You will be glad you did!"

—**John Stetson**, *America's Master Mentalist*,
The Stetson Experience

"*The Vitruvian Square* is a step-by-step journey into a new world of divination. Scott not only provides you with detailed and fascinating explanations for using Tarot and oracle cards with his mystic matrix, he literally shares with you an actual roadmap to enlightenment. Get *The Vitruvian Square* and let Scott guide you through new realms that will spark your imagination and add more power and meaning to your readings."

—**Kelli Maroney**, Actor (*Fast Times, Night of The Comet, Ryan's Hope, True Blood, One Life to Live, etc.*)

"Combining ancient mystical traditions, Renaissance art, tarot, spiritual alchemy, numerology, colors, letters, and Western Hermeticism, Scott Grossberg's *Vitruvian Square* offers a unique and parsimonious tool that provides a comprehensive understanding of the human condition and its place in the larger cosmos. Erudite, clever, insightful, and hugely practical, you will never be the same after reading this book and using the square for your own reflections and those of others. It is the Emerald Tablet of our age!"

—**Todd Landman**, *The Academic Magician*

"Scott Grossberg has written a must-have book for anyone interested in divination and mystical self-discovery. *The Vitruvian Square* is not only inspiring . . . it will make you think differently about oracles. This is the divination book you have been waiting for from someone you can trust."

—**Pamela Nine**, Professional Intuitive Counselor

Praise for *The Vitruvian Square*

"I have used Scott's *Vitruvian Square* system for years. This unique system adds so much more depth and interest to my tarot readings, not to mention my clients find it FASCINATING. Scott has put so much thought and detail into *The Vitruvian Square*. I highly recommend it!"

—**TC Tahoe**, *The 33rd Most Interesting Man in the World*, award-winning magician, Tarot reader

"A new book brings a glint of scales on the edge of its pages. An old book returns a river to the mouth. For ten years, Scott Grossberg's *Vitruvian Square* has been lending us the shimmering of chance by establishing a grammar common to all divinatory systems. This is how we learn that oracles are formal problems that, seen with eyes clean of superstitions, make readable the poetry of life. This is a book about the possibilities of possibilities, delivering the mystery of clarity."

—**Enrique Enriquez**, Author, Tarot Historian

"By all accounts and reviews since its original release, the impact that *The Vitruvian Square* has had on the readings and mystical community is evident. It has become an influential book. Given the wealth of other studies with which we can refer, I do not make this claim lightly. However, as I have developed further into this area across the years, I have found that the perspicacity of the principles are so profound and concentrated within, that they can speak deeply on many levels; both within the flow of the application of readings, as well as the appreciation of synchronicities beyond. You also have the ability to transform someone's life into something truly mystical and wonderful. Study this well. Read it all, or skip around, but refer back to it often."

—**Steve Drury**, *Inner Rapport Publishing*, Psychological Magician, Author

"Through the discoveries of his *Vitruvian Square*, Scott Grossberg can show you an already-present esoteric connection of virtually every past divination technique, in one easy-to-learn treatment. With a numerological 'engine,' he delightfully shares with you a clever and novel system that can connect anyone to his or her subconscious self. I predict you will love this!."

—**Alain Nu**, *The Man Who Knows*, mentalist, television personality, Las Vegas headliner

THE VITRUVIAN SQUARE

*A Handbook of Divination
and Mystical Discoveries*

10th Anniversary Edition

SCOTT GROSSBERG

⌘

ANCIENT MAGIC PUBLISHING

ALSO BY SCOTT GROSSBERG

The Most Magical Secret – Four Weeks to an Ecstatic Life

The Most Magical Secret Action Guide

The Deck of Shadows

The Masks of Tarot – Betraying the Face of Illusion

The Discovery Meditation

Visions – A Masterclass in the Magic of Fortune Telling

Proper Tarot – The Beginner Course

The Shunyata Code – An Answer to Finding Calm in Stressful Times

The Magic of Divination - 7-Day Challenge

The Seven Keys – Unlocking the Past, Present & Future

The Million Dollar iPad

The iPad Lawyer

THE VITRUVIAN SQUARE
A Handbook of Divination and Mystical Discoveries
10th Anniversary Edition

scottgrossberg.com

Publisher: Ancient Magic Publishing

ISBN: 978-0-578-74093-5

1. Fortune Telling 2. Tarot 3. Numerology 4. Divination

Second Edition: November 2020

First printing edition November 24, 2010.

Published in the United States of America.

For more information, send email to: sgrossberg@hotmail.com

or write to:
Scott Grossberg
700 E Redlands Blvd, Ste U-161
Redlands, CA 92373

FOR CAROLYN—

You continue to take my breath away.

CONTENTS

FOREWORD
TO THE 10th ANNIVERSARY EDITION

"A system that contains all systems."

"The last book that you will need on this matter."

"This is the only place you could both begin and end your study of how to give accurate, meaningful readings."

Hyperbole? You would be forgiven for thinking that. Especially in a world where so much is hyped beyond its real worth. However, in this case you would be wrong.

These are all things I have said and am happy to stand beside when talking about Scott Grossberg's wonderful book, *The Vitruvian Square*.

My relationship with Scott goes back for the best part of a decade. In 2010 he visited London, and lectured for 'Psycrets', a society of mystery performers, of which I was a member. To my disappointment, due to other commitments I could not make it to that meeting, but the chatter afterwards from members was incredibly positive, and in the years that followed many continued to speak of that particular meeting with great fondness.

Scott's oracle deck, *The Deck of Shadows,* and his earlier book, *The Masks of Tarot* with its Hiding Places system of giving a reading made a big impression.

I finally got to meet Scott when he attended a professional hypnotherapy training I hosted in Las Vegas in 2012. Despite it being our first face-to-face meeting, he greeted me like an old friend, and we connected immediately. Our friendship has deepened ever since.

Scott's experience with hypnosis and human change is almost as deep and long as his connection with magic and mystery - yet despite this, his enthusiasm to learn new things and test them out remains undimmed. His commentary and feedback on our approach added nuance and refinements that enhanced my work.

I experienced some of Scott's real word magic that week, too. He has a wonderful ability to ask powerful questions of you that can lead to personal transformation. Questions that you may not immediately be able to answer; questions that go to work on you, that won't go away, that burrow into your psyche, and only later provide an astonishing revelation.

After this, I began to study Scott's work deeply. Firstly, the system he shared in *The Masks of Tarot*, and later *The Vitruvian Square*.

Both offer exquisite examples of his very particular kind of genius, but it is *The Vitruvian Square* that must be considered his masterwork. It is, as I have said, 'the system that contains all systems.'

Learn this one, and with or without your preferred divination device, you will have the ability to tell people about themselves and so much more.

It is systematic yet retains fluidity. It provides structure yet remains vastly spacious. It gives you a map that enables you to explore freely.

The power of *The Vitruvian Square* should not be underestimated. It will enable you to connect with others in a way that is deeply felt, thought-provoking, and emotionally-charged. *The Vitruvian Square* is a book that I know you will treasure and return to repeatedly. Each time that you do, like a crystal turning in a beam of light, showing its facets off one by one, it will reveal more of itself, so that you may reveal more of others.

Scott Grossberg is what I call a 'proper genius.' One that I am honoured to share ideas with and delighted to call my friend.

— Anthony Jacquin, *The Hypnotist*

FOREWORD
TO THE FIRST EDITION

Welcome to *The Vitruvian Square.*

Knowing what I know, I envy your position now and I'm thrilled about the incredible journey and path upon which you're about to step foot.

Many months ago, I contacted Scott Grossberg to seek his advice on something that had been deeply troubling me. Extremely impressed with Scott's live readings and radio performances, his former works, *The Masks of Tarot* and *Bauta,* and his oracle cards, *The Deck of Shadows,* I was certain I had contacted the proper man for this particular issue.

At the time I had recently crossed over from doing readings with one oracle (system, method, and approach) into new and uncharted territory that was foreign to me on the level at which I was practicing. I had fallen flat on my face multiple times now, HARD, and I didn't want that to happen again.

I realized immediately that I had to grow, adapt, evolve, and then expand my tools and refresh my approach to what I call *The Art and Science of Knowing Other People.*

There had to be an answer and I was confident that Scott Grossberg had it, knew of it, or could point me in the right direction to find it. I couldn't have been more correct!

I contacted Scott out of pure necessity and we spoke for some hours about the special problems and issues I was experiencing. Besides providing me with volumes of priceless insights and invigorating approaches to what I was doing, Scott told me there was something else he had been working with privately for several years now . . . something he called, *The Vitruvian Square.*

Little did I realize that Scott was actually tipping (for the very first time) HIS OWN superb system and approach for giving deep and impactful readings; a system composed of equally balanced parts built and maintained with a sort of elegance and harmony only a Master could deliver. What appeared then was a systematic approach to the "art of knowing others" – a cohesive structure, path of logic, and school of wisdom (as functional as any oracle could provide or hope to offer) which not only allowed for one's natural knowing, intuition, and creativity to flourish, but the system itself demanded and provoked such.

Though he had developed his system quietly and for his own private use, Scott was willing to provide me with a basic write-up of his unique system and got to work. What appeared over the following weeks and months was a multitude of insights, methods, techniques, and approaches that were nothing short of *ABSOLUTELY BRILLIANT.*

Once Scott had started the amazing task of putting his thoughts and approach into words, he often found it difficult to stop writing as this particular system flows so organically from one insight to the next that each piece explained and opened up the doors wide to a dozen others. Interestingly enough, this is exactly what will take place in your own readings drawing upon *The Vitruvian Square* system.

What Scott shared with me has completely transformed the way I do my readings. No other technique or approach I've ever used has been of such incredible value or personal benefit to me and even my clients can tell the difference. My level of confidence has soared, my private readings and public performances have become tighter than ever before, and I'm simply able to KNOW MORE with far less time and effort.

Using the approach and methods Scott has honed and perfected through years of personal use, you'll find yourself ready and able to give amazingly detailed readings in any situation or venue, without repetition, without stock lines or memorized scripts, without the need for chicanery of any kind and without fear of failure.

If there's <u>one thing</u> I've learned in all my years of doing this work, I owe the most self-growth to and personal success in the realm of private readings and public question answering, it is without a doubt Scott Grossberg's *Vitruvian Square.*

Having derived such remarkable value and insight, confidence, personal power, and sustained ability from this approach I gently encouraged Scott and nudged him in the direction he had been contemplating in private, specifically, making this work available to others.

That Scott's *Vitruvian Square* had impacted me on such deep and significant levels was more than enough to convince me this was something others could and would greatly benefit from, as well. For me personally, Scott's approach was the missing link in my own work and provided me and the people I read for exactly what was being sought after, needed, required, and desired to take my readings and our experience together to the next level and beyond.

What started as a private sharing and conversation between friends has evolved into what I firmly believe will be hailed as the single greatest advance and breakthrough approach to giving readings developed in the last 100 years.

Though Scott has offered us a superior system, rock-solid approach, and spectacular structure to implement in our readings it should be noted this is NOT a "cold reading" method. Like every oracle born through necessity, *The Vitruvian Square* provides us with a combination of tools (all working together) which allows the reader, the client, the oracle, and the individual parts that comprise each to move the experience and insights gleaned from one point and level to the next in an elegant, logical, intuitive, detailed, and harmonious fashion.

Scott's approach is an even blend and perfect balance between logic and intuition. Once you've learned and integrated *The Vitruvian Square* system, you'll be able to look at a person, place or thing, question, problem or circumstance, and through interacting with the square, be able to know and understand it on a deeper and more profound level than ever before.

That nothing in this field or endeavor has been of greater value or personal significance to me speaks volumes. Through Scott's approach I am better equipped to truly *"Know Thyself"* and now I see *The Vitruvian Square* in all things. It is the perfect looking glass, sounding board, and reflective surface within which one is allowed and empowered towards a level of understanding and intimacy rarely approached. More than just an incredible system for giving readings, *The Vitruvian Square* provides us with a tool and process for self-discovery.

My own work with *The Vitruvian Square* has shown me more and more every day that our world is made up of symbols, layers, energies, codes, thoughts, consciousness, suggestions, perceptions, and our feeble attempts to define and make sense of these things. And though we may never fully understand all of them, we CAN begin to understand all of them even more via the work and process you're currently holding.

Enter now the *Vitruvian Palace* and allow her residents to speak to you. In a short time you'll begin to see *The Vitruvian Square* in all things, and that all things exist (on some level) within *The Vitruvian Square.*

By throwing yourself and/or another person into this self-contained Palace of Wisdom you'll see things you've not ever seen before . . . and it will happen very quickly.

To end, I'm absolutely honored that Scott has shared this ground-breaking work with me and even still, that I'm able to write the forward to this book. It will go down in history as an instant classic and the gold standard by which all future systems and approaches shall be measured.

Grateful,
Jerome D. Finley

THE VITRUVIAN SQUARE ™

0

BEING
REMEMBERING

KARMA/SPIRIT
FOOL

GOLD

ULTIMA MATERIA

PRIMA MATERIA

	PLANE OF OUTCOMES Future Choices Consequences	PLANE OF VALUES Present Opinions Beliefs	PLANE OF DUTY Past Memories Blame	

PLANE OF THOUGHT
 	
Mental
Will
Thought
	1 AJS
	BEGINNING
	RENEWING
	
	MAGICIAN
	WHEEL
	SUN
	    RED
		2 BKT
		CONNECTING
		RECONNECTING
		
		H. PRIESTESS
		JUSTICE
		JUDGEMENT
		    ORANGE
			3 CLU
			CREATING
			RECREATING
			
			EMPRESS
			HANGED MAN
			WORLD
			    YELLOW
				Negative:
				Unfocused
				Careless
				Thoughtless
				Dreamer

PLANE OF PASSION
 	
Emotion
Desire
Feeling
	4 DMV
	BUILDING
	REBUILDING
	
	EMPEROR
	DEATH
	    GREEN
		5 ENW
		CHANGING
		REPLACING
		
		HIEROPHANT
		TEMPERANCE
		    BLUE
			6 FOX
			UNITING
			REUNITING
			
			LOVERS
			DEVIL
			    INDIGO
				Negative:
				Insensitive
				Uncompassionate
				Aversion
				Touchy

PLANE OF ACTION
 	
Physical
Sensation
Skill
	7 GPY
	DEFEATING
	RETAKING
	
	CHARIOT
	TOWER
	    VIOLET
		8 HQZ
		MOVING
		REMOVING
		
		STRENGTH
		STAR
		    BLACK
			9 IR
			COMPLETING
			REFINISHING
			
			HERMIT
			MOON
			    WHITE
				Negative:
				Inertia
				Inaction
				Detached
				Ungrounded

AXIS OF POWER — Ability / Control

AXIS OF PROTECTION — Armor / Security

Negative: Insecurity Attack Unguarded

Negative: Impotent Inability Helpless

Negative: Carefree Unreliable Unprepared	Negative: Skeptical Disbelief Unopinionated	Negative: Absolution Forgetful Prideful

THE PLAY OF WISDOM

Wisdom begins in wonder.

- Socrates

Since mankind's earliest days, we have sought to know the thoughts of another. From the sheer need for safety and survival, we have tried to predict what tomorrow will bring. The challenge, of course, has been how unique we all are and the different ways each of us has tried to know and understand ourselves and what waits for us up ahead. No one dreamt it would be possible to bring all the varied divination methods together into one workable system. Until now . . .

Reduced to its simplest description, this is a book about fortune telling. Really, this is a book that teaches you how to tell people about themselves, where they have been, and where they are likely going. Inside these pages you are given a system of techniques that have been joined

together in a novel and highly useable way.

So, are you ready to embark on an exciting and mystifying

adventure through the world of prediction and prophecy?

To see how easy *The Vitruvian Square* is to use, look at the

opening diagram in the book and, with a pencil, make a mark in each

square that contains a letter of your name. For example, using just my

first name (you can use your full name if you'd like to), I place a mark in

square "1" (S), a mark in square "3" (C), a mark in square "6" (O), two

marks in square "2" (T-T). If you're going to use your full name,

continue to make marks in the appropriate squares for each of the

remaining letters.

When you are finished, just take a moment and look at the

patterns the marks reveal. Notice if some squares have more marks than

others – the locations that exclaim, "I am here – honor me and you will

be rewarded." Take the time to actually see which Tarot cards, alchemical

symbols and colors are emphasized by the shapes that have emerged.

Observe, too, the squares that are vacant and seem to cry out, "Did you

forget about me?"

This is but one of the many ways the information in this book can be used. There is something inside waiting to appeal to everyone's liking. If nothing else, the one thing this book promises is to fulfill the expectations of those who come to visit you as a reader – within these pages you will be given the ability to provide distinct and specialized "readings" to anyone, at any time, and under any conditions.

What follows are the keys to easily and instantly putting ancient wisdom to work for you. So, keep reading and discover the secrets and meanings of . . .

The Vitruvian Square!

INTRODUCTION
TO THE 10th ANNIVERSARY EDITION

When fortune calls, offer her a chair.

- Yiddish saying

How quickly ten years have passed. And, yet, how appropriate that *The Vitruvian Square* is celebrating its tenth anniversary - a number that brings us back around to the beginning (10 = 1 + 0 = 1 = Unity/Beginning). And so, I find myself re-creating a passion project that has found new friends around the world and allowed me to travel and lecture and share in places that are as enchanting as this book.

   The Vitruvian Square, to a certain degree, was gifted to me. It arrived, as most magical things do, in a flash of direct revelation. I was doing a Walking Meditation and contemplating the Lo Shu Square when the nuances you find in this book were given to me. For those who don't know, the Lo Shu Square is a 3x3 matrix of numbers and arises from the pre-historic story of a magical turtle emerging from flood waters. The turtle's shell contained a pattern of dots in a 3x3 grid that came to be known as the Lo Shu pattern. The top line of the Lo Shu pattern, as it is used in more contemporary times, consists of the numbers 4, 9, and 2. The second line is comprised of 3, 5, and 7. The third and final row holds the numbers 8, 1, and 6. The sum of each row, column, and diagonal in the Lo Shu Square equals 15, an uncanny symmetry that over the centuries has led it being deemed a truly *magic* square.

My use of *The Vitruvian Square* goes well beyond divination. It has become a way of seeing the world, people, and events. Many of you have already heard me describe the system as a unified theory of divination. Having used this matrix for over a decade, I can now tell you that it is also a unified theory of creation. Those who use *The Vitruvian Square* receive a new way of observing time, events, actions, and energy patterns. It is, to put it another way, a blueprint that allows you to access different dimensions of your consciousness and understanding.

In our modern world, we have become so accustomed to divination following rules laid down by others. However, in the more distant past, divination was practiced through the singing of words, inspiration and impressions, the welcoming of visions, the holding of dreams and the actual appreciation of day-to-day omens. What you will find in these pages are techniques for rediscovering the old way of doing things so that you, too, can both "sing the fates" and discover some of the secrets of the Universe. Indeed, each time I use *The Vitruvian Square* it's as if new levels of understanding are peeled away. I invite you to do your own meditations upon the system, the physical construction of the matrix, and the implicit symbolism of the correspondences.

For this reason, I also invite you to expand *The Vitruvian Square* to accommodate your own beliefs, philosophies, practical needs, and the expectations of the people for whom you read. It is a dynamic structure. Indeed, this expanded 10th Anniversary edition has content that was unearthed as part of my continuing evolution with and education by my own use of *The Vitruvian Square*. To put it another way, what I thought was going to be a complete reading system has turned into an otherworldly teacher of sorts that keeps poking and prodding to thrive and flourish.

My work with *The Vitruvian Square* continues to evolve. I'm sure even more waits to be discovered. By me. And by you.

HOW TO WORK WITH THIS BOOK

The Vitruvian Square is built upon profound and concentrated principles. At the very least, I recommend that you study the foundations on which the matrix is built. This means paying particular attention to Parts Two, Three, Four, Five, and Six. Reflecting on these chapters will give you information about *The Vitruvian Square* basic numbering system, the use of letters with the matrix, how to apply the Major Arcana of the Tarot to each square, the various planes that exist within the structure (the Planes of Outcomes, Values, Duty, Thought, Passion, and Action), and the two axes (the Axes of Power and Protection). Understanding these will arm you with enough information to use *The Vitruvian Square* quickly and in a straightforward fashion.

Once you have these fundamental structures in mind, you can then jump around within the book as might fit your needs and interests. If you are more inclined to use *The Vitruvian Square* in a meditative and mystical way, you can jump right into Parts Eleven (Mythic Readings), Twelve (Medicine Wheels and Structures of the Self), Thirteen

(Alchemy), Nineteen (Additional Tools), Twenty (*The Vitruvian Palace*),

Twenty-One *(The Vitruvian Labyrinth)*, and Twenty-Two (The "I am

Peace" Ho'Oponopono Prayer). If you want to start using *The Vitruvian*

Square for powerful and exciting readings, I invite you to jump into Parts

Eight (Choosing The Squares to Use – The Basics), Nine (The Threefold

Number Method), Ten (Further Adventures), Fifteen (The I-Ching), and

Eighteen (Palmistry).

    Of course, you don't have to jump around within the book, at all.

Indeed, you will find that the chapters are laid out in a type of journey

that leads you from one concept to the next. You will also notice that

there are twenty-two parts to the book and there are twenty-two cards in

the Major Arcana of the Tarot. You have, then, a sort of monomyth

quest in these pages; an adventure that takes you through various stages

of learning and experience.

    While specific attention has been paid to the use of Tarot cards

and my own *Deck of Shadows* oracle deck, any prophetic tool can be used

with this system. Indeed, that is the very reason that I've referred to *The*

Vitruvian Square as a unified theory of divination. Use your imagination.

Use the tools you have at hand. Create new associations. Create new

correspondences. Have fun. Play with the matrix.

May you find that *The Vitruvian Square* enhances how you already approach life. May you find that *The Vitruvian Square* deepens your realization and appreciation of the synchronicity of everyone and everything in your life. May you start to notice that your readings take on a deeper meaning and help to bring your sitters to a more meaningful path through the Universe.

Peace.

INTRODUCTION
TO THE FIRST EDITION

I do not know what I may appear to the world,

but to myself I seem to have been only like

a boy playing on the sea-shore,

and diverting myself in now and then finding

a smoother pebble or a prettier shell than ordinary,

whilst the great ocean of truth lay all undiscovered before me.

- Sir Isaac Newton

Different methods of using and presenting divination are plentiful. There

appear to be as many unusual and dissimilar ways of giving "readings" as

there are unique personalities in this field. Just look around and you see palm readers, card readers, crystal gazers, people who cast stones and coins and sticks and bones, and the tellers of a star's alignment. Some eclectically combine the many schools of thought. Others - the purists - maintain their chosen divinatory proficiency is the true path. And beginners are often undirected and confused as they flounder in trying to find the "best" system; the divination artifacts that "call" to them.

As I started writing this, I often asked myself, "Do we really need another book on divination? Isn't it just simpler for the experienced reader to make up a new spread or technique or just rediscover something explored when first starting out? Wouldn't it be more prudent to politely direct the novice to any number of self-proclaimed and well-meaning introductory (and perhaps over-generalized) books at the local bookstore or online retailer?"

Then I was drawn back to my pleasure at discovering that this apparent diversity of tools, rituals, and techniques may actually conceal a simple starting point and the implications of that breakthrough. Within these pages you will find evidence of the real unification and connection of seemingly distinct fortune telling and alchemical schemes. Play with me for a time as you imagine there is an overlooked or long forgotten unity in all acts of foretelling. Just suppose there is really a fundamental, underlying, and central framework from which all readings can be born and then transformed; a deeper, consistent, and inherently familiar pattern that readily produces and invites experimentation and personalization.

If my own insight is correct - and it has certainly proven experientially to be so through innumerable readings, workshops and performances - then *The Vitruvian Square* system I present in these pages offers three things to my readers:

1. For the novice - here is an easy-to-understand, easy-to-use starting point for those wanting to learn to do any type of reading. There is no doubt, however, that it would be helpful if the beginner has some initial background in Tarot symbols and meanings.

2. For experienced readers - here is an aesthetically consistent and elegantly powerful method for bringing your current reading skills to the next level and merging what you already know with ancient knowledge.

3. For intuitives - here is a fresh approach to focusing your instincts and inner knowing that produces uniform and empowering perceptions and understanding.

From a personal perspective, *The Vitruvian Square* concept was simply designed to give rise to more accurate and mysterious readings, predictions, and insights for a wider range of people and in a full spectrum of settings (face-to-face, radio, stage, television, online conferencing, etc.). Additionally, I crave variety. *The Vitruvian Square* offers an assortment of reading choices while keeping an intimate and comforting connectedness with rudimentary principles to fall back upon, if needed.

Within these pages I know you will enjoy the ideas, unfolding mysteries, and symbolism that we explore together. Even better, once you learn the basic concepts for *The Vitruvian Square*, you will have a strong groundwork upon which you may build a lasting and rewarding practice.

So . . . take some private time now and let this book act as a medium between your visible and spiritual worlds. Allow me to share some magical knowledge and wisdom that will ultimately provide you with intensely useful divinatory tools whether you are just starting out on your "reading" adventure or you are already a prophecy superstar.

To understand *The Vitruvian Square* fully and how to apply it for readings, this book is organized to first give you some history and background from which *The Vitruvian Square* was developed. I will explain how and why the ancient Lo Shu Square was modified, how Tarot cards and other oracles complement and confirm *The Vitruvian Square's* layout, and outline the basic numerology that will fuel your readings.

Next, I will spend time showing you how the different types of numbers and letters can be used to give your readings eerily accurate direction. I will also explain the various planes and axes – the directions – that the various numbers and letters can occupy during a reading and what those mean. A full discussion of the ways in which the Major Arcana from the Tarot is also given to you since these serve as archetypes that lend undeniable depth to your interpretations. I will also provide you with an understanding of the assorted patterns that can be created with the places that make up *The Vitruvian Square*.

With this background established, you will next be given instructions on actually using *The Vitruvian Square* for readings – how to choose the squares to be read, how to interpret names and dates, and how to use assorted oracle devices to enhance the reading experience.

Next, I will discuss more expanded and esoteric uses for *The Vitruvian Square*. Among other things, you will be treated to a lively discussion of Alchemy and how alchemical principles can easily be practiced. You will be shown how to create readings using RPG dice, sacred geometry, and a concept called "The Platonic Solids." You will also be presented with a way to create Mythic Readings using Joseph Cambell's idea of the *Hero's Journey*. Then you will be gifted a discussion and outline of using Medicine Wheels with *The Vitruvian Square's* layout.

Next, I will show you some miscellaneous odds and ends – curious and singular techniques for using *The Vitruvian Square* to answer "yes and no" questions, methods for imbuing color into your readings, and the use of palmistry and astrology.

Finally, there are some little diversions provided for your enjoyment; methods that involve the creation of magical seals, the use of incantations, and a journey through a *Vitruvian Palace* for empowerment and inspiration.

I find that this order of presenting *The Vitruvian Square* materials is the most practical and permits you, the reader, the most logical evolution of the concepts. Let us begin, then, our discovery of the remarkable predictive power of *The Vitruvian Square*.

PART ONE
SOME BACKGROUND

All things come out of the One and One out of all things.

- Heraclitus

Think of *The Vitruvian Square* as an orphic union of the well-established Lo Shu Square with the various correspondences and imagery of numerology, colors/chakras, medicine wheels, and Tarot. It is a once-secret blending of alchemical magic and past wisdom. For me, it has become the technique of foretelling and prophecy that I use whenever I am asked to give a "reading" as it provides me with a method for giving completely propless talks.

The Vitruvian Square has a varied and cryptic bloodline. It is as much founded on the sciences of sacred geometry, Vitruvian harmony, and Da Vinci's "Cannon of Proportions" as it is based on the arcane and esoteric arts of inspiration and divination, including the ancient Chinese "Lo Shu Square." I hasten to note that it is more than a bare reimagining of previously published methods with a few items moved around for novelty's sake. Rather, I consider *The Vitruvian Square* as a coherent and fresh predictive structure that is consistent with conventional divination theories and well-established symbolic, alchemical, and numerological meanings.

By way of history, and with respect to The Lo Shu Square and its "simple" and Yantram variants, much has already been written about using them for fortune-telling. From a purely visual orientation, the greatest difference between the Lo Shu and *Vitruvian* Squares is the placement of the numbers. The original Lo Shu Square had the numbers 1 through 9 placed, as follows (Figure 1):

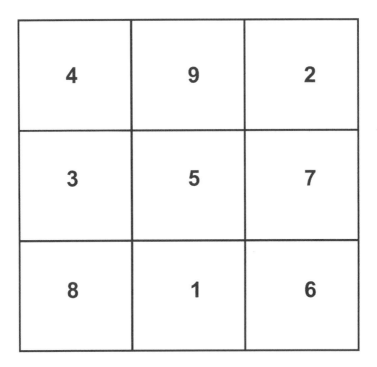

**Figure 1 - Original Lo Shu Square
Configuration**

The pattern we know today as the Lo Shu Square was, according to Chinese legend, discovered nearly 4,000 years ago by Emperor Yu on the back of a turtle shell. The original Lo Shu Square is said to have been comprised of yin and yang symbols or dots. The diagram above (Figure 1) is a modern version using standard number notation in place of the yin/yang dots.

You will note that the traditional Lo Shu Square is actually what is known as a "magic square." In other words, if you add up the numbers in each of the three rows (4-9-2, 3-5-7 and 8-1-6), in each of the three columns (4-3-8, 9-5-1 and 2-7-6), and in both diagonals (4-5-6 and 2-5-8), each one totals 15.

The usual, simplified Western variant of the Lo Shu Square (Figure 2) takes away the "magic square" configuration of the original numbers and reorders them in the following easy-to-remember sequence:

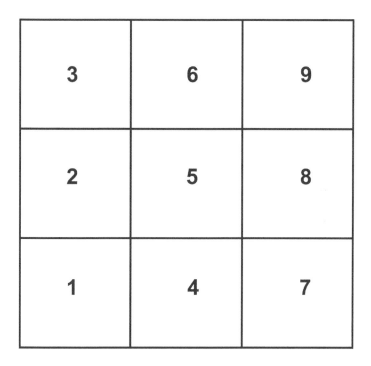

**Figure 2 - Western/Simplified Lo Shu
Square Configuration**

From this modified Lo Shu square model, numerologists were able to make patterns of the rows, columns and diagonals and attribute meanings to those conventions. It is important to note that neither the traditional nor modified versions of the Lo Shu Square utilize the number "0" during the calculations.

With *The Vitruvian Square* (Figure 3) you take the foregoing design and gracefully shift it one clockwise turn so that the numbers are now arranged in the following pattern:

0

1	2	3
4	5	6
7	8	9

Figure 3 - The Vitruvian Square
Basic Configuration

Unlike its predecessors, *The Vitruvian Square* also adds the number "0" to its design at the very top. This will permit us to vastly expand its practicality and use. This new constellation of numbers allows a more ordered, coherent, and refined association with the various divinatory systems we commonly know and love. Moreover, this updated alignment provides a polished means for applying alchemical dimensions and the fourfold pattern of Jung's human archetypes we have come to know as "King, Warrior, Magician and Lover."

The Vitruvian Square, in addition to owing its numerical content to Chinese numerology, obviously has a form that arises from the concept of Sacred Geometry and the works of Pythagoras of Samos, Marco Vitruvius Pollio, and Leonardo Da Vinci. Indeed, the Pantheon in Rome was a structure designed to respect and pay homage to "all the gods." The Pantheon's patterns (Figure 4) served as some, if not all, of the inspiration for Da Vinci's iconic "Vitruvian Man" drawing (Figure 5).

Figure 4 - Ceiling of the Pantheon (Photograph by Scott Grossberg)

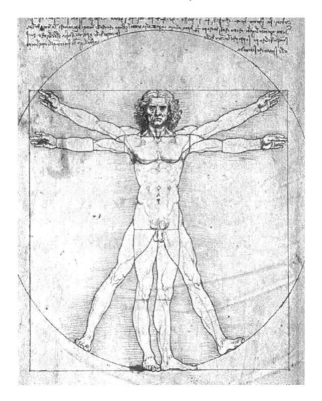

Figure 5 - Da Vinci's "Vitruvian Man"

The Pantheon's name comes from the Greek language and means "every god" and it was dedicated as a structure for "all the gods." *The Vitruvian Square* is, likewise, tendered as a sibyllic guide to be used with all divination systems. Similarly, as Da Vinci's "Vitruvian Man" with its ideal human proportions was meant to demonstrate how the human body was an analogy for the universe, so too *The Vitruvian Square* is intended to show the precise placement of the numbers and patterns they reveal are an analogy for the universe of predictions.

So that you can truly value what the subtle clockwise shift of the modified Lo Shu Square means, look at the first image located on page 12 at the beginning of this book – the one of *The Vitruvian Square* with the "Vitruvian Man" image in the background. You will see that the "Vitruvian Man's" proportions fit completely and without qualification into the square pattern. Most importantly, the various planes and axes embedded in *The Vitruvian Square* scheme are true companions with the human body as depicted by Da Vinci and described by Vitruvius.

As further investigation of the path I was taking with this system, I looked for validation in the imagery of the Tarot. What I found was gratifying. I specifically narrowed my focus on the portion of The Magician Card (Figure 6) that contained the body language of The Magician from the original Rider-Waite-Smith[1] design:

---

[1] The cards were drawn by Pamela Coleman Smith based on instructions and input from A.E. Waite. The deck was published by the Rider Company. Thus, the deck became known, among other names, as the Rider-Waite-Smith deck.

**Figure 6 - The Magician Tarot Card from
Rider-Waite-Smith Deck (c. 1909)**

The Magician (Card 1 in the Tarot deck) is, among other things,

the one who freshly takes from above and manifests below. He begins

with his right arm raised and ends with his left hand pointed to the

ground. Now, look at the same card with *The Vitruvian Square* overlaid

upon it (Figure 7):

**Figure 7 - The Magician Tarot Card with The
Vitruvian Square Overlay**

You can see how The Magician starts at the number "1" (the
number of firsts and beginnings) and ends at the number "9" (the
number of completion and ending). It was from this marrying of
concepts that *The Vitruvian Square* was finally realized. You can also see
there is a diagonal created by The Magician's outstretched arms across
squares 1, 5, and 9. This is what I will describe later as the "Axis of
Power." These observations also served as the basis for the various axes
and planes that will be used for more thorough readings.

Now I must digress here for those of you who use the Tarot de Marseille or similar Tarot decks. I am aware that these decks have some different orientations for their archetypal drawings. As you will see in Figure 8, Le Bateleur (The Magician) from the Tarot de Marseille deck, has his left arm raised and his right arm downward. He also looks to his right rather than straight ahead.

Figure 8 - Le Bateleur from The Tarot de Marseille (c. 15th cent.)

Le Bateleur's arms align along what will later be described as the "Axis of Protection" (squares 3, 5, and 7) rather than the "Axis of Power" (squares 1, 5, and 9 as we found with The Magician from the

Rider-Waite image). This, of course, leads to a different underlying interpretation for and driving force behind Le Bateleur because, using the Axis of Protection as our reading foundation, we see one who executes his magic for tribute and security. Having briefly addressed this situation, I confess that I have been unabashedly selfish in using only the Rider-Waite imagery to demonstrate and accompany the balance I found between the various forms of divination and *The Vitruvian Square's* configuration.

Returning to the Rider-Waite designs, let's look at The High Priestess (Figure 9) with the square overlay as another example of how Tarot integrates so well with *The Vitruvian Square*:

**Figure 9 - The High Priestess Tarot Card with
The Vitruvian Square Overlay**

The High Priestess takes her position and fixes her gaze upon you from her home at the number 2 position. Of course, you can also see that she is suitably balanced through the three verticals (planes) created by connecting the squares at 1, 4, and 7 then 2, 5, and 8, and finally 3, 6, and 9, as well.

Let's explore one more example so that you can then search on your own for the hidden meanings that await discovery. The Tarot card Strength (Figure 10) in play with *The Vitruvian Square* looks like this:

Figure 10 - The Strength Tarot Card with The Vitruvian Square Overlay

The first thing I notice about this interaction of the original card's image (body language) and the Places of Power is the diagonal that runs from square 1 down to square 9 (the Axis of Power). You then have the strong base of squares 7, 8, and 9 (the Plane of Action). I note that both the Plane of Outcomes (squares 1, 4, and 7) and the Plane of Values (squares 2, 5, and 8) are covered. Finally, the Strength card starts in the Plane of Thought.

Commenting on some of these observations, the Axis of Power addresses the need to command and facilitate achievement. That is precisely what the Strength card talks to us about – that by using our mental prowess and intensity (Plane of Thought) we are able to control

(Axis of Power) the effects and imports of the material and fleshly things

around us (Plane of Action). The fact that Strength lies in both the

present (Plane of Values) and the future (Plane of Outcomes) is self-

narrating. Indeed, Strength primarily lies in the present squares while

having influence on the future.

Some of the cards you will examine and meditate upon on your

own will afford easy analysis. Some will require you to delve deeper and

look for hidden treasure; additional "reading" tools that will undoubtedly

give voice to things you have subconsciously felt but not previously

noticed.

As I indicated earlier, with *The Vitruvian Square*, the number 0 is

placed outside the primary squares of power and at the very top. This

number (represented by The Fool in the Tarot deck) symbolizes and acts

as The Soul and Karma. The Fool in the Rider-Waite deck is shown as a

young man about to step off a cliff without an apparent care in the

world. He is innocence incarnate as he lightly steps out into his new

adventure. The Fool (Le Mat) card in the Tarot de Marseille deck depicts

a man on journey, looking up at the heavens, and letting the stars guide

him. Like The Fool, the number 0 move everything else forward.

PART TWO
THE BASIC VITRUVIAN SQUARE

All things, at least those we know, contain Number;

for it is evident that nothing whatever can

either be thought or known without Number.

\- Philalaos of Tarentum

In Part Eight, I will show you the various Places of Power within *The Vitruvian Square* to be used. Before that, however, it is important that you understand the basic attributes of the square.

0
BEING

1 BEGINNING	2 CONNECTING	3 CREATING
4 BUILDING	5 CHANGING	6 UNITING
7 DEFEATING	8 MOVING	9 COMPLETING

Figure 11 - The Vitruvian Square Basic Numbering System

At the heart of *The Vitruvian Square* is the application of and correspondence between numbers and the various places of power inherent in *The Vitruvian Square's* design. The basic square associations (Figure 11) are built around standard numerological meanings. Thus, 1 is the "beginning" up through 9 which is "completing." You can also think of the journey from number 1 through number 9 as a mythological story or the stepping-stones for each person's life; each number having a different personality and characteristic. These meanings are intended as guidelines for you and not meant to be used exclusively or in a strict manner. Draw your own inferences from the meanings and correspondences that I provide.

To start our understanding of how individual numbers are used in *The Vitruvian Square*, let us first agree on a basic understanding of two shapes that make up the numbers 1 and 0. These two figures serve as the cornerstone for the interpretations of all the numbers we will be discussing.

ZERO - 0

0 has been described as representing: the Void, the Infinite, Gestation, Unformed Creativity, the Limitless Space, the Unknowable, No-thing, something that is boundless, Truth, Purity, Love, Everything, and the Alpha and Omega. As the sphere of universe, it is something of unfixed proportions. In Eastern philosophy it has also been described as the "void of unattachment," "the golden womb," and "the first egg." At the same time, it is both the infinitely bountiful and the immeasurably small.

0 relates to the Major Arcana card of The Fool. It is the power of choice and of all things being possible. It is the force that comes from receiving, giving back, and fulfilling.

Keywords: boundless, unlimited, infinite, non-attachment, and a movement upward. 0 presents an opportunity to be more than you already are and to grow into that which you are supposed to be. It is something that is outside the normal range of number and does not play the game encompassed by 1 through 9.

0 is a gift we are given when the time is right and the proper combination of other attributes and principles have been followed.

ONE - 1

1 is the beginning. A single, simple line (perhaps the infinite loop of 0 has been subdued and now has a focused course); it grows and manifests from the earth (the ground) upwards to the heavens. Alternatively, it is a single bolt of energy rousing from the firmament and shooting down to earth to reveal itself. It represents an extremely active principle. 1 also looks like "I" – perhaps no coincidence since the Minor Arcana "ones" represent the ego, assertion, personal creativity, potential, beginnings, and being ready for action. It is the previously discussed 0 brought into existence and made evident, apparent, and demonstrable.

Keywords: individuality, new beginnings, opportunity, self-reliance, distinction, innovation, separateness, and expression. The number 1 also relates to the Major Arcana cards of The Magician (I), The

Wheel of Fortune (X) (10 = 1 + 0 = 1), and The Sun (XIX) (19 = 1 + 9 = 10; 10 = 1 + 0 = 1). While 1 is the beginning of a cyclic journey, 10 also represents the need/desire/want to start over after fulfilling a cycle.

Simply, 1 is the power to give and seduce, as well as the weakness of immersion.

TWO - 2

If you look at the number 2 you can envision that it is a combination of a 1 (lying on its side) and half of a 0. In other words, the straight line that normally transverses heaven and earth is now lying down and earthbound. This baseline is a foundation on which other things build. The power of this number comes from the earthly plane. The upper part of the 2 is infinity (0) split open. This gives us the "potential" to touch the infinite more than the actual "means" of achieving it. Notice that the fragmented 0 is open to its right indicating this is a number that reacts from and to future events.

2 also represents the philosophical concept of dualism – the doctrine espousing that reality always consists of two opposing elements. Thus, 2 is the number of relationships and unification and agreement. This is a force that results from blending and combination.

Keywords: balance, flexibility, partnership, relationships, attraction, duality, alternation, a cross-road, duplication, and harmony.

Bear in mind that 2 can also be a dilemma. It may present itself as the feelings of uncertainty and not being able to choose between the limited options of only two things/options/people. 2 relates to the Major Arcana cards of The High Priestess (II), Justice (XI) (11 = 1 + 1 = 2), and Judgement (XX) (20 = 2 + 0 = 2). It is the power of resolution and partnership, as well as the weakness of indecision.

As a hint of things to come, look at the 2 and you can also see how the 5 can be seen as a 2 turned upside down.

THREE - 3

The number 3 looks like a 0 hinged open – just as if it is getting ready to give birth to something. As such, the number 3, when used in conjunction with the Tarot, has been described as the full expression of the particular suits (Wands, Cups, Swords, and Pentacles). To put it another way, 3 is the expression of "family" (father, mother, and child). You can also see how 3 looks like half the potential of 8. As such, 3 can be thought of as the opposite of 8 with the two being dangerous to each other.

3 may also be viewed as a pair of nurturing breasts (similar to the letter "B" discussed later in the book and as described by Enrique Enriquez). It is the number of choice (as opposed to being faced with the dilemma that is the number 2). And don't forget the sayings, "Third time's a charm," and "Three strikes and you're out." 3 also represents the model of the physical universe or three-dimensional space (length, width, and depth/height).

Keywords: creation, optimism, increase, achievement, volition, extension of the self, expansion, and growth. 3 relates to the Major Arcana cards of The Empress (III), The Hanged Man (XII) (12 = 1 + 2 = 3), and The World (XXI) (21 = 2 + 1 = 3). It is the power of nourishment and affection, as well as the weakness of starvation.

FOUR - 4

4 is a number of things and people joining and establishing a firm foundation together. Look at it and you can envision the number 1 with a hand reaching out and up to the heavens. It also looks like a triangle atop the number 1. Irrespective of which image you choose, both invoke feelings of seeking and using divine power to create firmness, experience, and knowledge here on earth.

Keywords: structure, order, stability, building, stagnation, experience, reality, materiality, and foundation. 4 relates to the Major Arcana cards of The Emperor (IV) and Death (XIII) (13 = 1 + 3 = 4). It is the power of things that endure and balance as well as the weakness of wanting more.

FIVE - 5

As mentioned earlier, the number 5 can be seen as the number 2 flipped upside down. This gives us a number that encompasses the concepts of conflict, loss, and need. The 1 is still turned on its side but now rests in the heavens (rather than on the earth as with a 2). The 0 is, once again, halved. As with the number 2, the fragmented 0 is open to its right side (the side representing "days to come") indicating this is a number reacting to and from things yet to be and promises of tomorrow. Because the bottom of the 5 is opening towards the earth – it is seeking grounding - the number 5 provides us the "means" of and the footing for achieving the infinite as more important than the bare "potential" for doing so. In other words, the process here is more significant than the actual outcomes. Both the numbers 5 and 2 can be seen as carrying forth or signaling possibilities but without essential action to implement those things. They are ambitious numbers. With 5 you are midway to the

complete reward of 10.

Keywords: instability, uncertainty, mediation, conflict, reward and

punishment, lost opportunities for change, interchange, exchange, and

conversion. 5 relates to the Major Arcana cards of The Hierophant (V)

and Temperance (XIV) (14 = 1 +4 = 5). It is the power of opposition

and resistance, as well as the weakness of incompatibilities.

As a side note, the English astrologer Sepharial (Dr. Walter Gorn

Old) observed that 5 is the only number that cannot be paired with

another number to total 10 or completion. As such, he described 5 as

"left behind, unpaired and unrelated."

SIX - 6

Just as the 2 and 5 are interrelated so, too, are the numbers 6 and

9. In this case, the 6 and 9 are both horizontal and vertical mirrors of

each other (alternatively, you can think of the 6 rotated 180 degrees

clockwise or the 9 rotated counterclockwise). 6 can be seen to be the

number 1 being born from a 0. This is the power of 1 arising from the

infinite. 6 is not just the magnitude of being without limits, it is the

possessing of qualities that enable you to do and be something. It is

about cooperation, connections, and twining. This is the number that promises a future firmly rooted from the past as can be seen by both the

0 and 1 coming from the number's left side (the side representing "things

that were").

Keywords: equilibrium, reciprocation, sympathy, communication,

problem solving, learning, connections, balance, alchemy, harmony,

restitution, and cooperation. The number 6 relates to the Major Arcana

cards of The Lovers (VI) and The Devil (XV) (15 = 1 + 5 = 6). Both of

these cards, by the way, depict a man and woman standing together; the

former showing the couple in love and overseen by an angel with the

latter showing the same couple but in chains and overseen by a devil.

This number is the power of prevailing and holding on, as well as the

weakness of needing to survive.

SEVEN - 7

The number 7 is a compounding of two 1's. One line leads

upwards to the heavens, thus signifying action. The other line, if you

imagine yourself as the number, extends to the right side (the Future) of

the first line and creates a horizon in the sky indicating things are quite

solid, sensible, and practical. You could also imagine the 7 as a 1

throwing a spear towards "something yet to be." All of these images

summon thoughts of possibility poised to spring into action.

This number represents the labor pains of creativity; the discontent of wanting something more because you can see, sense, and feel victory about to happen. This is the number of creation triggered by intentional change. 7 represents the ability to "go the distance" but still needing to go through challenges and quests.

Keywords: victory, perfection, assessment, motives amplified, equilibrium, agreement, and a soul developed. 7 relates to the Major Arcana cards of The Chariot (VII) and The Tower (XVI) (16 = 1 + 6 = 7). It is the power of struggle and strenuous effort, as well as the weakness of conflict.

EIGHT - 8

The number 8 is not just the sign for infinity turned upright. It is also two 0's - one atop the other. As such, you have the embodiment of the Hebrew phrase, *L'olam Vaed*. You know the phrase in English as "forever, and ever" – not just the concept of something endless, but the re-emphasizing and underscoring of "always" and "enduring." This is the image of infinite possibilities literally stacked on top of each other. Go back over the discussion of the image of 0 and you will see it is greatly increased here.

Of course, the danger in 8 is the chance you might do nothing more than go around "spinning your wheels"; creating the appearance of movement without any real action being taken. Thus, while the number 8 can represent the actual movement into a solution, it runs the risk of dissolution, as well. In other words, the indulgence that 8 brings with it also bestows the termination of things the way they were.

Keywords: earthly progress, invention, reconstruction, inspiration, interconnection, self-mastery, movement, action, change, and power. 8 relates to the Major Arcana cards of Strength (VIII) and The Star (XVII) ($17 = 1 + 7 = 8$). It is the power of a change in position and things made real and concrete, as well as the weakness of doubt.

NINE - 9

The number 9 is a 6 rotated 180 degrees. This is the infinite (0) holding on and trying not to float away as our "1" rises to the heavens. This is an image of the infinite departing the earth while leaving a remnant behind.

This is the number of leftovers, renewal, and recompense. It is the number of a debt being repaid.

Keywords: transformation, endings, attainment, disuniting, and fruition. 9 relates to the Major Arcana cards of The Hermit (IX) and The

Moon (XVIII) (18 = 1 + 8 = 9). It is the power of richness, being filled to capacity and volume, as well as the weakness of things slightly inadequate and not quite accomplished.

TEN THROUGH TWENTY-ONE

For those times when you want to use the numbers 10 through 21 in order to correspond with the Major Arcana cards from the Tarot or you essentially want to use the same squares of power again with more intensity (as can happen when you are using a person's name or a date to find emphasized squares) - it is a simple matter of adding "re-" to each of the key concepts just outlined. As you know, "re-" means to do something again. By using "re-" with the original squares' meanings, you are adding more mightiness, more passion, and more effort to your focal point.

Thus, the basic square can now be expanded (Figure 12), as follows:

0 BEING REMEMBERING		
1 BEGINNING RENEWING (10, 19)	2 CONNECTING RECONNECT- ING (11, 20)	3 CREATING RE-CREAT- ING (12, 21)
4 BUILDING REBUILD- ING (13)	5 CHANGING REPLACING (14)	6 UNITING REUNITING (15)
7 DEFEATING RETAKING (16)	8 MOVING REMOVING (17)	9 COMPLETING REFINISH- ING (18)

Figure 12 - The Vitruvian Square Expanded Numbering System

To aid you in your own further exploration of these additional numbers, let's explore how the number 10 might be used.

The number 10 is all things; you have both the 1 and 0 in all their glory. The 1 and 0 appear independent of each other and, yet, for this number to form, they must act in concert. This is the number of culmination, conclusions, and reward. With 10 it is not as much about what you do, as about experiencing the final results of your past. With the number 10 you have started over again and re-established yourself like new (and, usually, improved).

Keywords: fate, freedom, completion, end of a cycle, and Karma. 10 relates certainly to the Major Arcana cards of The Magician (I) and The Wheel of Fortune (X), and also to The Sun (XIX) (19 = 1 + 9 = 10). It is the power of bestowed honor, strength from rewards, reincarnation, and recognition, as well as the weakness of perfection.

You can readily see how the mere inclusion of the "additional" concepts of 10 through 21 provides you with an entirely new playing field that you might not previously have thought about. Indeed, most numerology studies don't include numbers beyond 9 (other than 11, 22 and 33). For the most part, they certainly don't include a discussion of 0.

Now you have additional tools. Rather than simply treating the number 11, for example, as a higher vibration of the number 1, you have concepts of renewal, reclamation, and replenishment to talk about. The number 12 is not just a more advanced version of the act of creating (3). It is manifesting all over again.

PART THREE
THE LETTERS OF THE ALPHABET

Whatever happens in our lives is of little importance.

What matters is how we tell the story of what has happened to us.

- Enrique Enriquez

Magic Squares, historically, provide you the ability to overlay the alphabet onto each number. Using these standard numerological associations with *The Vitruvian Square* (Figure 13), we have:

1 A, J, S	2 B, K, T	3 C, L, U
4 D, M, V	5 E, N, W	6 F, O, X
7 G, P, Y	8 H, Q, Z	9 I, R

Figure 13 - The Vitruvian Square Basic Lettering System

When *The Vitruvian Square* is used to analyze names and words, one of the most potent and fulfilling analyses for interpreting letters comes from an inspirational and magical friend by the name of Enrique Enriquez. Enrique is a renowned Tarot reader and author, in his own right, and resides in New York. He used to maintain a blog called "tarology" which was amazing. That blog was eventually turned into various books that I encourage you to explore. A documentary about Enrique's approach to the Tarot – *Tarology: The Art of Tarot* – was also produced back in 2013.

Within Enrique's webpages was buried a short and masterful treatise entitled, "the game of seeing®." When Enrique's thoughts were shared with me, the following was inspired and is now offered with Enrique's generous permission.

In utilizing these letters, you can take someone's name or an event title or even a thought and apply the individual letter's qualities. Thus . . .

A

The letter "A" has its feet firmly spread and planted on the ground. It is anchored and primed for action while being reactive to the material things around it. The letter's head points heavenward like an arrow shooting into the sky while there is an anchoring of passion and emotion across its mid-section. This is the first letter of the alphabet and, thus, is the epitome of the concept of "beginnings."

Keywords: A new beginning, strong balance, solid instincts, a sharp head, and worldly-minded.

B

Enrique says that when the letter "I" grows arms to grab itself it becomes the letter "B." It can also be thought of as "two milky breasts" full of nourishment and sustenance. It can also be seen as "two protruding eyes wanting to see it all" or "two arms holding a treasure against its chest." There is a sense of selfishness and clinging to the letter "B."

Keywords: Sustaining, nurturing, nourishing, and self-interested.

C

The letter "C" is an "I" that has curved at the top and bottom towards the past (its left side). As such, this letter is open and receptive to the influences and vibrations of a time gone by. As sensory and absorbing as "C" is, it is always waiting to be occupied and made full. As such, the letter "C" is always incomplete.

Keywords: Not yet finished, candid, receptive, and admissive.

D

The letter "D" is an "I" that has become pregnant with its own possibilities. Notice that it is facing towards its left, however; a reminder that what is about to develop has its roots in the past. This is the letter embracing the creative principle made reliable.

Keywords: Ability, significant, implication, and expectant.

E

The letter "E" is the letter "I" with arms and legs extended through all three planes (thought, passion and action). This is the letter of conjuration and fancy because "E" is able to dabble on all three planes of existence. "E" is seeking "something out there" in the external world. "E's" ability to reach a final climactic stage, however, is illusory as it is always drawn back to its immobile spine. It is the letter "B" without the ability to actually join things together or make itself complete or the letter "B" that has exploded open so that its energy is discharged.

Keywords: Fantasy, play, call forth, engage, illusion, and elaboration.

F

The letters "F" and "P" are related. With our "F," it can be thought of as an "E" that is missing its Plane of Action or a "P" whose head has burst and its thoughts scattered. In other words, this letter operates from the heart and in the clouds and wants to act but ultimately lacks the anchoring to make it complete. The letter "F" also runs the risk of falling down if it is not careful.

Keywords: Absent, lost in thought, dreamer, and visionary.

G

The letter "G" is a "C" pointing at itself. This letter, then, is egocentric and generally concerned with its own needs and wants. It may, as Enrique imparts, also suggest that "we dispel any false sense of wholeness by performing an act of attention which will take us back inside ourselves." Enrique continues that the letter "G" says, "looking within is a way to be reborn over and over."

Keywords: Divine selfishness, aware, mindful, care, and tending.

H

The letter "H" looks like a staircase or ladder with a separation from "above" and "below." As Enrique astutely notes, this letter can also be seen as two "I's" joining forces and moving towards the heavens. The two-columned body of the letter "H" denotes a movement upwards. Yet, the horizontal line at the heart level is a reminder that there is a hierarchy of things that exists when one is standing up straight.

Keywords: Erect, structure, ascension, rising, and direction.

I

The letter "I" is similar to the number 1. Both of them can be made from one single upright stroke of the pen. They represent the individual, distinctness and ability. From the letter "I" all other letters can be formed just as the number 1 serves as the beginning of all our numbers. It also reminds us to stop and consider where we are, where we have been and where we are going.

Keywords: Individuality, importance, power, knowledge, and stopping.

J

The letter "J" is an "I" with a hook on the bottom; a sharp curve that keeps the "J" stuck in place and unable to rise higher. "J" faces its right side, however, indicating that it continues to look forward and to the future – even if it is unable to immediately get there.

Keywords: Amazed, bound, confined, mortal, and temporal.

K

The letters "K" and "R" are similar. When you read the full explanation of "R," below, you will see the letter deals with "theory in action." While the "R" has a rounded top half (the expectation of something happening), the "K" is open – like two arms reaching outwards. Thus, with "K" we have someone who is both reaching and moving towards a desired outcome. Note that both the "K" and "R" are oriented, or facing towards their left sides, which indicates a retreat or drive into the past if deemed necessary. Likewise, their backs or stems are stiff and staked in the present with no indication that a move into the future will happen anytime soon.

Keywords: Accomplishing, attaining, extending, and impervious.

L

The letter "L" is an "I" standing up with an additional "I" on its side. Perhaps the bottom extension of the "L" is the shadow cast by the main "I." The horizontal elongation and expansion rests in the Plane of Action – the area of the material and physical world. Thus, this rooting in the material world –this standing ground - keeps the otherwise strength of the individual "I" from fully forming and being noticed. This letter is not addicted nor caught by the earthly plane like the letter "J." Rather, "L" simply balances on the world of sensation and skill as it finds the earth an easy pillow. The letter "L," unfortunately, is a mindless and heartless path.

Keywords: Resistance, holding firm, strong, steady, and elaboration.

M

The letters "M" and "W" are related as they are the vertical, mirrored reflections of each other. Dealing with "M" for the moment, the letter looks like two mountains with a valley in between them or perhaps two letter "A's" holding hands but they are missing their midsections. "M," then, is the letter of ups and downs – those periods of positive and negative events, people and things. This is the letter of shifting moods and emotions.

Keywords: Aroused, extremes, challenges, stimulation, and passion.

N

The letter "N" is made up of two upright "I's" with a diagonal running from the future (the letter's right side) downward to the past (the letter's left side). This is the act of descension, of coming down but perhaps not all the way to one's lowest point. Unlike the "M," there is no rise back to the top, again. With the letter "N" you have two "I's" keeping their distance from each other.

Keywords: Aloofness, moving downward, remoteness, and indifference.

O

The letter "O" resembles the number "0." Both, then represent non-attachment, infinity and oneness. Here is the universe and the concept of movement around a path. As Enrique writes, "the 'O' says, 'being and becoming are one single thing.'" The letter "O" can also be a bottomless pit for the unwary or careless for it is so attracting.

Keywords: Unguarded, uncommitted, eternity, unending, and spinning in circles.

P

The letter "P," like the "F," has its head in the clouds. It also looks like a flag either waving as a herald on its way into battle or a place marker for a chosen locale. However, our "P" is now like the "D" and the "R" (described below) as the top half is closed and full of prospects and conceivability. As Enrique describes "P," it is an "F" whose heart and mind joined in order to become whole.

Keywords: Herald, idealist, dreamer, announcement, and declaration.

Q

The letter "Q" is our "O" with a "J"-like tail. Thus, we have eternity snared by the material world. Or, perhaps, this is timelessness finally giving birth. Even further, maybe this is a balloon wanting to break free of the world but being held here by the slimness of a string.

Keywords: Escape, flight, entrapped, and deliverance.

R

As first mentioned with the discussion of "K," look at the "R" and you will see that it appears to be someone getting ready or trying to move. This is a letter preparing to "take off." The upper half of the letter is, like the letter "D," full of possibility while its lower half is like the letter "A"; legs spread and standing on the material plane. Unlike the "A," however, our "R" is active. "R," then, tells us of a journey or travel that is about to begin - at least the person for whom you are reading thinks he or she is moving "forward." As a reminder, the "K" and "R" are facing towards their left sides indicating a willingness to withdraw into the past. The rigid supporting stem is rooted in the present with no indication that a move into the future will happen anytime soon.

Keywords: Motion, crusade, lift off, setting forth, journey, and acceleration.

S

"S" is our chameleon letter. It is an "I" curved from the present to be open to both the past and the future simultaneously. It is all things to all people at all times. The letter "S" is fluid, changeable and sometimes inconstant. It is very balanced and versatile. This letter connects heaven and earth in a continuous two-way dialogue. It is also a "whip-like lightning bolt" reaching from the heavens to the earth –

something that can be both nourishing and destructive.

Keywords: Changeable, volatile, ceaseless, balanced, and

exchange.

T

The letter "T" is two "I's." One is upright and frozen in the

present. The other is horizontal – laid on its side – and spread across the

past, present, and future in the Plane of Thought almost like a hat

protecting the rest of our "T" from too much exposure from above. This

is a letter that shows what happens when one reaches an intellectual limit.

This is also a letter of tranquility and silence – a reminder for "looking up

from time to time." The letter "T" may also have started out as one

horizontal line in the realm of the mind and thought that is now

manifesting down to earth having reached its capacity above.

Keywords: Stillness, quiet, waiting, shelter, call down, and invoke.

U

The letter "U" is an open vessel or cup receptive to and waiting

to be filled from above. It is opportunity and chance. Perhaps it is the

container from which an alchemist can mix his potions to accomplish his

Great Work. Because of its rounded bottom, it may tilt and wobble from time to time, but it does not fall down. However, the letter "U" in its cuplike fashion may be filled with inspiration yet keeps its contents in check and will not spill them and infuse the earth with intuition and arousal.

Keywords: Open-minded, fortune, adventure, possibility, and shifting.

V

The letter "V" – a close relative to "U" – is carefully balanced in the present and in the earthy plane. While its antapex point represents a dynamic and active interaction with the earth, it could easily tip over but for the equilibrium it carefully wields. Its sharp point at the bottom does not yield any extension and keeps the letter isolated from outside influences. You will notice that the "V's" arms are moving up and away from its point in an opposite direction while the point, itself, might act like a funnel channeling celestial energy earthward. As Enrique points out perhaps the letter "V" is an upside down and heartless "A."

Keywords: Risk, peril, insulated, set-apart, fighting, and channel.

W

The letter "W" can be two "V's" or a flipped "M." As duplicative "V's" the need for careful balance disappears and, instead, the sharpness of the base of the letter becomes stabilizing and incisive. As an upside down "M" the letter "W" becomes the highs realized after a period of abrupt changes.

Keywords: Depression, a low point, penetrating, and acute.

X

We've all heard the saying, "X marks the spot." That essentially summarizes the letter "X." It is the center of all things – the crossroads – as the four corners converge in the middle. Enrique is quick to point out, however, that our "X" can also expand in all directions. The "X" can also be thought of as someone with arms and legs fully expanded and embracing the experience of "As above, so below."

Keywords: Junction, crossing, enlargement, treasure, and value.

Y

The letter "Y" is the letter "I" with its "head split open." It is also half of the letter "X" and shows us a letter that is being receptive to outside influences while maintaining a skeptical attitude. The letter "Y" can also appear as the funnel of a "V" with the contents focused and pouring out to the earth.

Keywords: Concentrated, refocused, yielding, opened, and redeemed.

Z

The letter "Z" is an "N" fallen on its side. As a result, we now have two horizontal lines; one in the Plane of Thought and one in the Plane of Action. The two lines are connected by a diagonal that follows the Axis of Protection. Thus, we have a letter that joins Heaven and Earth, but only through service to others. As with the "N," the diagonal line keeps the "I's" separated (or, in some cases, connected when they might not otherwise be so).

Keywords: Diminished, defensive, overprotective, restrictive, and enabling.

Once again, I am very grateful to Enrique for allowing me to share and expand upon his visions.

PART FOUR
TAROT – THE MAJOR ARCANA

Each man is a hero and an oracle to somebody.

- Ralph Waldo Emerson

Earlier we explored how a few Tarot cards can be applied to the

configuration of *The Vitruvian Square*. By continuing onward with this

construct, we arrive at the following Major Arcana associations (Figure

14):

0
FOOL

1 **MAGICIAN** **WHEEL** **SUN**	**2** **H. PRIESTESS** **JUSTICE** **JUDGEMENT**	**3** **EMPRESS** **HANGED MAN** **WORLD**
4 **EMPEROR** **DEATH**	**5** **HIEROPHANT** **TEMPERANCE**	**6** **LOVERS** **DEVIL**
7 **CHARIOT** **TOWER**	**8** **STRENGTH** **STAR**	**9** **HERMIT** **MOON**

Figure 14 - Major Arcana Tarot Associations for The Vitruvian Square

To help you in using these Major Arcana cards with *The Vitruvian Square*, here are some basic attributes and meanings for the various cards in their numbered positions. For a more in-depth examination of the Major Arcana, you might enjoy my book, "The Masks of Tarot," which can be used as a hearty supplement to what you find in the following pages.

In the following descriptions I am also giving you a glimpse of some of the alchemical concepts that will be developed in a later chapter.

0

The Fool (0) - He is the ultimate decision maker and the one who moves everything through time. He can appear anywhere (hence the number 0) and be completely at home. In the context of *The Vitruvian Square*, The Fool is all about being in the moment and simply existing. In an alchemical setting, he personifies the Ultima Materia (the reborn self) or Philosopher's Stone (the magical child). When the number 0 is used more than once in a reading, The Fool moves beyond "being" and represents someone who is rethinking, recalling, and retrieving memories.

1

All of the 1 cards represent beginnings or renewals in some way. They also represent, in Alchemy, the Primal Mud or the fertile substance from which creation is born. Each of these cards have numerical values that add up to 1.

The Magician (I) – The Magician is the first card encountered as we enter the body of *The Vitruvian Square*. He is the start of the creative process and the spark that brings things into reality. He creates existence. The Magician is also the passageway or conduit for a greater ability.

The Wheel of Fortune (X) ($10 = 1 + 0 = 1$) – Fate, as it is also known, is an event or course of events that are first put into play in the past and which necessarily occur in the future. The Wheel may also be viewed as the concept of Karma; the prior effects of a person's life being renewed in the present for a particular purpose.

The Sun (XIX) ($19 = 1 + 9 = 10$; $10 = 1 + 0 = 1$) – The Sun, among other things, represents the beginnings of our youth and all the joy and happiness we experienced. It is also the attempt to regain or renew that same joy in the present and to have it continue into the future.

2

All of the following cards stand for the concept of connecting –

the acts of putting together two or more things and people, making

logical conclusions, and bringing things and people together, again. In

Alchemy, this is the number of the primary element Earth.

The High Priestess (II) - The High Priestess navigates by joining

her subconscious and conscious minds. She is also the archetype of

opposites and secrets. Thus, The High Priestess is well-suited for the

number 2.

Justice (XI) (11 = 1 + 1 = 2) – Justice is all about finding fairness

and balance. It is concerned with what is perceived or actually is "fair."

Justice dictates that well-reasoned decisions (those made without excess

or extreme) will result in a conformity with rules and standards.

Judgement (XX) (20 = 2 + 0 = 2) – This card, among other

things, represents the rewards of self-contemplation and one's own soul-

searching; a re-finding of one's self. It is also about the embracing or union of divine wisdom and the end of delusions.

3

Number 3 cards represent events, people and things that support conception and the act of creating again. The alchemical equivalent of this is the essential of Salt or, in other words, these cards present themselves as the manifestation of the body and the birth of the physical being.

The Empress (III) - The Empress is all things living and the nurturer of mankind. She is the inspiration and mother of activity and situations.

The Hanged Man (XII) (12 = 1 + 2 = 3) – While The Empress is all about nourishment and sustaining, The Hanged Man is the self-sufferer who has surrendered so much of himself to and for others and their causes that he is in jeopardy of losing his distinctiveness. He is the one who will suffer death, if need be, for the sake of his world.

The World (XXI) (21 = 2 + 1 = 3) – The World is, by its very name, the materialization of that which is actual and real. This card also symbolizes the ever-present and changing experiences that are born throughout one's lifetime.

4

Number 4 cards all speak about building and rebuilding – of permanence, stability, and certainty. Their alchemical equivalent is the primary element of Water and the concepts of purity and cleansing.

The Emperor (IV) – We all want our ruler to be unsullied and pure for he is not only the ruler of the world but the expression of power for all those with whom he has contact. The Emperor stands for stability as he is certain of his place in creation.

Death (XIII) (13 = 1 + 3 = 4) – Nothing has more apparent permanence or guarantee than Death. And nothing brings cleansing and purging more than the demise of a prior way of thinking or consciousness. Death, with its scythe symbolism, reminds us that with every end there is a rebirth into something even more beautiful, knowing, and elevated.

5

The Number 5, as with these cards, is about change and transposition. It is also about putting things back – back in order, back in time, and back in position. It is both a return and a moving forward. From an Alchemy perspective, these cards are the conjunction or meeting place of all the others and then lead to an upward movement towards the completed soul.

The Hierophant (V) - The Hierophant is the focal point for creating his heaven on your Earth. He is the one who oversees his earthly congregants and brings them into the presence of that which he deems to be holy.

Temperance (XIV) (14 = 1 + 4 = 5) – As I have written about in "The Masks of Tarot," it is easy to confuse the cards of Justice and Temperance inasmuch as we instinctively want to believe that "rightfulness" and "equilibrium" are identical. Temperance, however, is a card about bringing all things together and achieving balance. This card represents the mixing together of ideas to form a harmonious whole.

6

Number 6 cards all correspond to the concepts of emotional and physical union, merging and reunifying; not just the bringing together of things, people and events but the actual flow and mix inherent in such a marriage. Alchemically, the number 6 equates with the prime element of Air. Accordingly, these cards contain the element needed to sustain life and which become very public displays of feelings and qualities.

The Lovers (VI) - The Lovers are, by their very title and nature, the paradigm for the concept of physical and emotional coupling. They represent not just selfish completion but the selfless desire and need to come together in a heavenly union; one of the most profound and impelling forces of mankind.

The Devil (XV) (15 = 1 + 5 = 6) – The Devil, in most cards, lords over a naked and chained man and woman – The Lovers. Their mortal union has been broken as much by their own doing as by outside forces. This card shows that a new coming together is necessary for them to obtain relief and ease.

7

The number 7 corresponds to winning victories and overcoming the odds. It is about recapturing and the act of taking something or someone back. In Alchemy, this pertains to the essence of Mercury or Quicksilver; the liquid fire that brings sudden and sometimes unpredictable outcomes but cannot stop its own nature.

The Chariot (VII) – The Chariot represents the seeking and achievement of a successful ending to a conflict. It is controlled by a driver who enjoys the battle as much as the return from the challenge.

The Tower (XVI) (16 = 1 + 6 = 7) – The Tower can be seen as the spoils that result from the assault and triumph of The Chariot. This card serves as a reminder that, like victory and Quicksilver, itself, nothing is permanent and change is an inevitable part of life.

8

The number 8 is the figure of movement and transference. In Alchemy, this is the Place of Power occupied by the prime element of Fire; the catalyst that initiates and accelerates other things, while also being the element that can alter and melt away that which is not wanted.

Strength (VIII) – Strength represents the deliberate and specific use of mental prowess to move away from or conquer a challenging situation. This favorable outcome is attained by the arousing and use of the mind.

The Star (XVII) (17 = 1 + 7 = 8) – All stars radiate energy as a result of their internal and external fiery reactions. With this card, The Star represents the vitality that hope and desire provide. The Star card is the promise of something better tomorrow; an archetype for moving away from today and into the future.

9

Our last number, 9, appropriately signifies completion, closure, and giving a new and fresh appearance to something that is not wanted any longer. In Alchemy this is the prime element of Sulphur; the abundant ingredient that both preserves and burns. Sulphur, according to Alchemists, is the heart or heat of a substance when viewed in context with other things. In other words, the following cards have their full meaning when viewed in relation to surrounding situations and events.

The Hermit (IX) – The Hermit card represents the leaving behind of one way of life for another. It is the decision that things have reached their point of culmination such that the only thing left to do is leave and start anew. This is a card about choices and leaving behind "what is" to find "what else there is."

The Moon (XVIII) (18 = 1 + 8 = 9) – The Moon appears to radiate only because it is viewed in the light of the Sun. Similarly, this is our subconscious, intuition, and imagination; those beliefs and feelings that are found through contemplation and observation of the world around us. This card, thus, represents the instinctive knowing when it is time to leave one home for another.

Both *The Vitruvian Square* and the Tarot represent the journey we make through Life. Indeed, we'll explore that in additional detail when we get to the discussion of *The Vitruvian Labyrinth*. Each Place of Power within *The Vitruvian Square* structure, as with each of the Tarot cards that occupy those locations, contain blessings and impediments. Take the time to explore how the associations in Figure 14 tell their own stories of desire, creation, adventure, challenge, hope, and recovery.

PART FIVE
THE PLANES

There are many paths to enlightenment.

Be sure to take one with a heart.

- Lao Tzu

Some authors, previously addressing the Lo Shu Square and other "magical" solids, have written about what they called the "Planes of Pythagoras." The general idea is a simple one; namely, when all of the numbers, letters or, in the case of Tarot, cards connect either an entire horizontal or vertical row there is special significance given to that range. Perhaps it's easier if you simply think of the various planes – what I call the Planes of Life in this book - as different layers of existence or growth.

Likewise, if a particular row or column is empty – in other words,
in doing a reading there are no numbers, letters, or cards in the
corresponding row's or column's Places of Power – that has import, as
well.

In *The Vitruvian Square*, the Planes of Life (Figure 15) and their
representing meanings look like this:

	PLANE OF OUTCOMES Future/ Choices Consequences	PLANE OF VALUES Present/ Opinions/ Beliefs	PLANE OF DUTY Past/ Memories/ Blame	
PLANE OF THOUGHT Mental/ Will/ Thought	1 AJS BEGINNING MAGICIAN WHEEL SUN	2 BKT CONNECTING H. PRIESTESS JUSTICE JUDGEMENT	3 CLU CREATING EMPRESS HANGED MAN WORLD	Negative: Unfocused/ Careless/ Thoughtless/ Dreamer
PLANE OF PASSION Emotion/ Desire/ Feeling	4 DMV BUILDING EMPEROR DEATH	5 ENW CHANGING HIEROPHANT TEMPERANCE	6 FOX UNITING LOVERS DEVIL	Negative: Insensitive/ Uncompassionate Aversion/ Touchy
PLANE OF ACTION Physical/ Sensation/ Skill	7 GPY DEFEATING CHARIOT TOWER	8 HQZ MOVING STRENGTH STAR	9 IR COMPLETING HERMIT MOON	Negative: Inertia/ Inaction/ Detached/ Ungrounded
	Negative: Carefree/ Unreliable/ Unprepared	Negative: Skeptical/ Disbelief/ Unopinionated	Negative: Absolution/ Forgetful/ Prideful	

Figure 15 - The Planes of Life within The Vitruvian Square

The Plane of Thought

The Plane of Thought is formed by connecting the squares numbered 1, 2 and 3. This row or level of creation focuses on mental activities, the mind, the will, and thought. The Plane of Thought is inhabited by the following Tarot Major Arcana: The Magician (I), The Wheel of Fortune (X), The Sun (XIX), The High Priestess (II), Justice (XI), Judgement (XX), The Empress (III), The Hanged Man (XII), and The World (XXI).

Each of the numbers, letters, meanings, and Tarot cards in this row involve conscious choice, decisions, and intentions as their primary strategies.

The lack of any numbers, letters or cards in the Plane of Thought indicates someone who is unfocused, careless, thoughtless, and someone who is a dreamer.

The Plane of Passion

The Plane of Passion is formed by combining the squares numbered 4, 5, and 6. This row is the level of creation that embraces emotions, desires, feelings, and hopes. These Tarot Major Arcana dwell within the Plane of Passion: The Emperor (IV), Death (XIII), The

Hierophant (V), Temperance (XIV), The Lovers (VI), and The Devil (XV).

Each of the numbers, letters, meanings, and Tarot cards in this particular row involve strong emotional responses to feelings and the outside world, the principles of right and wrong, and the experiences of the heart as their primary strategies.

The lack of any numbers, letters, or cards in this row indicates someone who is insensitive, uncompassionate, and "touchy." This is someone who turns away from things.

The Plane of Action

The Plane of Action is formed by combining the squares numbered 7, 8, and 9. This row is the level of creation that finds its best footing with those things in the physical realm, sensations, and skill sets. The following Tarot Major Arcana comprise the Plane of Action: The Chariot (VII), The Tower (XVI), Strength (VIII), The Star (XVII), The Hermit (IX), and The Moon (XVIII).

Each of the numbers, letters, meanings, and Tarot cards in this row require the use of the body, some physical aspect or drive, or elementary stimulation as their primary strategies.

The lack of any numbers, letters or cards in this row indicates someone who has a predisposition to be inert and someone who is inactive, detached, and ungrounded.

The Plane of Outcomes

The Plane of Outcomes is formed by combining the squares numbered 1, 4 and 7. This column exists in the level of creation that projects from the Future and casts its charms through the allure of choices and consequences. The following Tarot Major Arcana comprise the Plane of Outcomes: The Magician (I), The Wheel of Fortune, (X), The Sun (XIX), The Emperor (IV), Death (XIII), The Chariot (VII), and The Tower (XVI).

Each of the numbers, letters, meanings, and Tarot cards in this column look to or are driven by the actions or events of the Future as the basis for what they do, feel, and think.

You will also notice that this column is the only one comprised of numbers made of straight lines. In other words, each of the Places of Power within the Plane of Outcomes is entirely made up of 1's. Look back on the descriptions of 1 and you will see why each of the items contained within this column thrives on individuality and distinct.

The lack of any numbers, letters or cards in this column indicates someone who is carefree, unreliable, and unprepared. This is also someone who does not care about the Future.

The Plane of Values

The Plane of Values is formed by combining the squares numbered 2, 5, and 8. This column exists in the level of present creation and lives in the moment through the play of opinions and beliefs. The following Tarot Major Arcana comprise the Plane of Values: The High Priestess (II), Justice (XI), Judgement (XX), The Hierophant (VIII), Temperance (XIV), Strength (VIII), and The Star (XVII).

Each of the numbers, letters, meanings, and Tarot cards in this column look to or are driven by judgments, sentiments, and faith of the present as the basis for what they do, feel, and think.

The lack of any numbers, letters, or cards in this column indicates someone who is skeptical, disbelieving, and unopinionated. This is also someone who does not care about the Present.

The Plane of Duty

The Plane of Duty is formed by combining the squares numbered 3, 6, and 9. This column exists in the level of creation we know as or believe is the Past. This is where we find perspective, comparison, and contrast through memories, the placing of blame, and the experience of shame. The following Tarot Major Arcana comprise the Plane of Duty: The Empress (III), The Hanged Man (XII), The

World (XXI), The Lovers (VI), The Devil (XV), The Hermit (VIII), and

The Moon (XIX).

Each of the numbers, letters, meanings, and Tarot cards in this

column look to or are driven by the eminence, conflict, and experiences

of the Past as the basis for what they do, feel, and think.

The lack of any numbers, letters, or cards in this column indicates

someone who is always forgiving, forgetful, and prideful. This is also

someone who does not care about the Past.

The Planes of Thought, Passion, Action, Outcomes, Values, and

Duty, represent the various internal and external driving forces that impact

our daily lives. These Planes, when viewed from the perspective of *The

Vitruvian Square*, can show the path that a particular individual has taken,

is taking, or is likely to take with a great degree of accuracy and sensitivity.

Using The Planes in conjunction with the other tools provided in this

book, you will be able to give specific reading insights that provide a deep

understanding of how we run towards and run from what we believe are

our successes and failures.

PART SIX
THE AXES

I like the dreams of the future better than the history of the past.

- Thomas Jefferson

An axis can be thought of as a "center" around which things rotate, turn on, or turn around. There are two primary axes in *The Vitruvian Square* (Figure 16). These are the influences and forces around which the various Places of Power spin their tales. They look like this:

AXIS OF POWER
"Ability/Control"

AXIS OF PROTECTION
"Armor/Security"

1 AJS BEGINNING MAGICIAN WHEEL SUN	2 BKT CONNECTING H. PRIESTESS JUSTICE JUDGEMENT	3 CLU CREATING EMPRESS HANGED MAN WORLD
4 DMV BUILDING EMPEROR DEATH	5 ENW CHANGING HIEROPHANT TEMPERANCE	6 FOX UNITING LOVERS DEVIL
7 GPY DEFEATING CHARIOT TOWER	8 HQZ MOVING STRENGTH STAR	9 IR COMPLETING HERMIT MOON

Negative:
Insecurity/
Attack/
Unguarded

Negative:
Impotent/
Inability?
Helpless

Figure 16 - The Axes within The Vitruvian Square

The Axis of Power

The Axis of Power is a diagonal line running from the top left corner (the Future) of *The Vitruvian Square* down to its lower right corner (the Past). As you will recall, this access is derived from the stance of The Magician Tarot card, whose right hand is lifted high into the upper leftmost cell of *The Vitruvian Square*, while his left hand is pointing down to occupy the lower right cell of the matrix. It is formed with the squares occupied by numbers 1, 5, and 9. This slant runs the gamut from beginning, through change, and then on to the end. It embraces the act of The Magician experiencing the fruits of his wizardry and then choosing to move on. It is Fate playing out its fortunes only to have destiny reflected back the way it came. It is The Sun eagerly radiating its happy rays until the beams of light are manifested by the very things they shine upon.

Each of the Places of Power along the Axis of Power are just that – power – controlling influences and forceful energies. The following Tarot Major Arcana comprise the Axis of Power: The Magician (I), The Wheel of Fortune (X), The Sun (XIX), The Hierophant (V), Temperance (XIV), The Hermit (VIII), and The Moon (XIX).

Each of the numbers, letters, meanings, and Tarot cards in this column look to or are driven by the need to exercise control over their worlds and make things happen as the basis for what they do, feel, and think.

The lack of any numbers, letters, or cards in this diagonal shows someone who is impotent, ineffective, and helpless.

The Axis of Protection

The Axis of Protection is a diagonal line running from the top right corner (the Past) of *The Vitruvian Square* down to its lower left corner (the Future). It is formed with the squares occupied by numbers 3, 5, and 7. This slant shows the range from creating, then change, and ultimately to defeat or destruction. It takes in the act of conception that only The Empress can bring, her nurturing of that which she has brought to life and then to her instincts for shielding others from danger. It is the Martyr who suffers to protect others and then sees the fruits of his abiding when the need for that misery is destroyed. It is The World in all its nourishing splendor providing a defense for its inhabitants through and against the cycles of time.

Each of the squares along the Axis of Protection are, in their own ways, representative of the desires to assist, defend, and nurture. Each wears its armor. Each provides security. The following Tarot Major Arcana comprise the Axis of Protrution: The Empress (III), The Hanged Man (XII), The World (XXI), The Hierophant (V), Temperance (XIV), The Chariot (VII), and The Tower (XVI).

The various numbers, letters, meanings, and Tarot cards in this diagonal render shelter, give tribute to what has been born and delivered, and are ever watchful for perils to those they love as the basis for what they do, feel and think.

The lack of any numbers, letters, or cards in this diagonal shows someone who is insecure, subject to attack, and unguarded.

Taken together, The Planes and Axes provide us with a profound understanding of some of the strong forces that continually act upon us. These forces move us on fundamental and temperamental levels.

PART SEVEN
OTHER CONNECTIONS

The important thing is not to stop questioning.

Curiosity has its own reason for existing.

One cannot help but be in awe when he contemplates

the mysteries of eternity, of life, of the marvelous structure of reality.

It is enough if one tries merely to comprehend

a little of this mystery every day.

Never lose a holy curiosity.

- Albert Einstein

The various planes and axes are the primary structures that I use with *The Vitruvian Square*. However, there are many more which you might find worthy of your attention: the Diamond of Harmony, the Square of

Chaos, the Triangle of Reflection, the Triangle of Results, the Cross of

Desire, and the Cross of Binding. If you are anxious to get started using

The Vitruvian Square right now, go ahead and jump ahead to Part Eight.

You can always return to this chapter after you have had some fun and

success giving *The Vitruvian Square* a workout. For those of you intent on

proceeding forward with learning the basics . . .

The Diamond of Harmony

1 AJS BEGINNING MAGICIAN WHEEL SUN	2 BKT CONNECTING H. PRIESTESS JUSTICE JUDGEMENT	3 CLU CREATING EMPRESS HANGED MAN WORLD
4 DMV BUILDING EMPEROR DEATH	5 ENW CHANGING HIEROPHANT TEMPERANCE	6 FOX UNITING LOVERS DEVIL
7 GPY DEFEATING CHARIOT TOWER	8 HQZ MOVING STRENGTH STAR	9 IR COMPLETING HERMIT MOON

Figure 17 - The Diamond of Harmony within The Vitruvian Square

The Diamond of Harmony (Figure 17) presents itself when the following even-numbered squares are covered: 2, 4, 6, and 8. This pattern speaks of the precious compatibility of one's opinions and one's actions. It is the treasured standard of agreement and congruence for it is, by definition, the lack of conflict and struggle.

The following Tarot Major Arcana comprise the Diamond of Harmony: The High Priestess (II), Justice (XI), Judgement (XX), The Emperor (IV), Death (XIII), The Lovers (VI), The Devil (XV), Strength (VIII), and The Star (XVII).

The various numbers, letters, meanings, and Tarot cards in this pattern, when present together, seek balance. They move forward searching for agreement between what they want and what they see, and they have the resolve not to give in when there is strife if yielding does not further collaboration.

The complete lack of any of these numbers indicate a person controlled or ignited by dissonance, dispute, and disagreement.

The Square of Chaos

1 AJS BEGINNING	2 BKT CONNECTING	3 CLU CREATING
MAGICIAN WHEEL SUN	H. PRIESTESS JUSTICE JUDGEMENT	EMPRESS HANGED MAN WORLD
4 DMV BUILDING	5 ENW CHANGING	6 FOX UNITING
EMPEROR DEATH	HIEROPHANT TEMPERANCE	LOVERS DEVIL
7 GPY DEFEATING	8 HQZ MOVING	9 IR COMPLETING
CHARIOT TOWER	STRENGTH STAR	HERMIT MOON

Figure 18 - Square of Chaos within The Vitruvian Square

The Square of Chaos (Figure 18) is created by the presence of the following odd-numbered squares at one time: 1, 3, 7, and 9. When these four locations are present simultaneously there is a tendency for confusion and disorder to arise because of the inbuilt struggles that subsist.

The following Tarot Major Arcana comprise the Square of Chaos: The Magician (I), The Wheel of Fortune (X), The Sun (XIX), The Empress (III), The Hanged Man (XII), The World (XXI), The Chariot (VII), The Tower (XVI), The Hermit (VIII), and The Moon (XVIII).

The various numbers, letters, meanings, and Tarot cards when brought together in this particular pattern work against each other. Their energies are in opposition and they become the unplanned foes of each other. On their own, dissension does not exist. In concert, however, they are their own worst enemies.

The complete lack of any of these squares in a reading, makes arrangements and associations possible.

The Triangle of Reflection

1 AJS BEGINNING	2 BKT CONNECTING	3 CLU CREATING
MAGICIAN WHEEL SUN	H. PRIESTESS JUSTICE JUDGEMENT	EMPRESS HANGED MAN WORLD
4 DMV BUILDING	5 ENW CHANGING	6 FOX UNITING
EMPEROR DEATH	HIEROPHANT TEMPERANCE	LOVERS DEVIL
7 GPY DEFEATING	8 HQZ MOVING	9 IR COMPLETING
CHARIOT TOWER	STRENGTH STAR	HERMIT MOON

Figure 19 - The Triangle of Reflection within The Vitruvian Square

The Triangle of Reflection (Figure 19) is created by the combination of the following squares: 1, 3 and 8. It is the "As above" part of "As above, so below." Think of it as the universe, itself, manifesting on Earth. When these three places of power are present in a reading, there are magical actions and intentions at play that, once believed in and acted upon, will reveal themselves in physical existence.

This is the realm of "belief" leading to experience.

The following Tarot Major Arcana comprise the Triangle of Reflection: The Magician (I), The Wheel of Fortune (X), The Sun (XIX), The Empress (III), The Hanged Man (XII), The World (XXI), Strength (VIII), and The Star (XVII).

The various numbers, letters, meanings, and Tarot cards when brought together in this particular pattern work together; first at the mental/thought/imagination level and then evince in the Plane of Action. This particular triangle represents the physical world being an outcome of vision and invention. Indeed, the square of power at number 8 (moving) is produced only after squares 1 (beginning) and 3 (creating) combine their intuitiveness and attention.

This arrangement shows what Creation and the Heavens have conspired together to present for you to ponder. It is what has had light cast upon it so as to be seen. It is the reflection of a person's Heaven on their Earth. When all of these squares are present in a reading, there is likely a situation that requires a reaction (as opposed to the attempt to control first). The complete lack of any of these squares indicates a situation where the person for whom you are reading is not taking charge or is ignoring their own imagination and intuition.

The Triangle of Results

1 AJS BEGINNING MAGICIAN WHEEL SUN	2 BKT CONNECTING H. PRIESTESS JUSTICE JUDGEMENT	3 CLU CREATING EMPRESS HANGED MAN WORLD
4 DMV BUILDING EMPEROR DEATH	5 ENW CHANGING HIEROPHANT TEMPERANCE	6 FOX UNITING LOVERS DEVIL
7 GPY DEFEATING CHARIOT TOWER	8 HQZ MOVING STRENGTH STAR	9 IR COMPLETING HERMIT MOON

Figure 20 - The Triangle Of Results Within The Vitruvian Square

The Triangle of Results (Figure 20) is created by the combination of the following squares: 2, 7, and 9. It is the "so below" part of "As above, so below." This formation bespeaks of the art of gaining a desired or yearned-for result from controlling and finalizing physical events, people, and things. In other words, here are our physical wants and needs ascending to Heaven and achieving a coveted materialization. This is the realm of experience and "reality" leading to faith and belief.

The following Tarot Major Arcana comprise the Triangle of Results: The High Priestess (II), Justice (XI), Judgement (XX), The Chariot (VII), The Tower (XVI), The Hermit (XIX), and The Moon (XVIII).

The various numbers, letters, meanings, and Tarot cards when brought together in this particular pattern work together; first at the carnal and fleshly level (what can be seen and touched) and then invoke oneness with the universe. In other words, skillful manipulation in the tangible world leads to effects in the Plane of Thought. As can be seen, the Place of Power at number 2 (connecting) is produced only after squares 7 (defeating) and 9 (completing) combine their triumph over and settlement/understanding of the physical world.

The complete lack of any of these squares indicates a situation where the person for whom you are reading is not taking charge or is ignoring his or her own imagination and intuition

The Triangle of Results is truly special in that it also yields a magical layout for any tangible divination device. Indeed, you can actually use this formation as a "magic spell" or mandala of sorts. If there is a particular "something" that you want to bring into existence for yourself or someone else, take my deck - *The Deck of Shadows* - or your favorite oracle (e.g., Tarot) and intentionally select three cards - one for each position of the triangle. You are not blindly pulling cards. On the contrary, you are choosing ahead of time which cards you want to see at each location. Then you are placing those specific cards in their locations for further consideration, meditation, and intention.

For example, Place of Power Number 2 will be occupied by the finest result you can imagine or desire. Places of Power Numbers 7 and 9 will be occupied by those forces/attributes/events you want to serve as the most elegant and excellent sources and/or causes for your outcome. When working with someone else, you can then ruminate and expound upon the choices of cards made.

When put together, the Triangles of Reflection and Results form, among other things, a hexagram (a six-pointed star figure) or two intersecting, mirrored triangles (a modified Star/Shield of David) (Figure 21):

Figure 21 - Combination of Triangles of Results and Reflection

These intersecting shapes taken together represent the entire concept of "As above, so below." You may think of this figure as representing the balance between Heaven and Earth or between the Universe/God and man.

The Cross of Desire

1 AJS BEGINNING MAGICIAN WHEEL SUN	2 BKT CONNECTING H. PRIESTESS JUSTICE JUDGEMENT	3 CLU CREATING EMPRESS HANGED MAN WORLD
4 DMV BUILDING EMPEROR DEATH	5 ENW CHANGING HIEROPHANT TEMPERANCE	6 FOX UNITING LOVERS DEVIL
7 GPY DEFEATING CHARIOT TOWER	8 HQZ MOVING STRENGTH STAR	9 IR COMPLETING HERMIT MOON

Figure 22 - The Cross of Desire within The Vitruvian Square

The Cross of Desire (Figure 22) is created by combining squares 2, 4, 5, 6, and 8. This formation, when present in a reading, indicates that the person for whom a reading is taking place, is responding to inclinations, hungers, and impulses rather than being overly cautious and premeditated. Don't be confused, however. This formation of squares is not about carelessness. Rather, this alignment reflects the granting of wishes and the successful operation of the Law of Attraction.

The following Tarot Major Arcana comprise the Cross of Desire: The High Priestess (II), Justice (XI), Judgement (XX), The Emperor (IV), The Hierophant (V), Temperance (XIV), (Death (XIII), The Lovers (VI), The Devil (XV), Strength (VIII), and The Star (XVII).

The various numbers, letters, meanings, and Tarot cards speak of bringing things together, building for the future, and then being secure in the face of shifting landscapes, emotions, and people. This is not as much about happy coincidences as it is a pattern that tells of a settled attitude and belief that all things happen for a reason. When these squares are present, the person receiving the reading believes that the Universe is conspiring for their own good. When all of these numbers converge and are present, you have an individual who is in a constant and current state of hope, trust, and want. They are less concerned with "what is" than with "what could be." They are unsatisfied - not necessarily in a spoiled way - but in a restless and dream-filled mood.

The complete lack of any of these squares indicates a person who is out of harmony with himself or herself; someone who finds things a "twist of Fate."

The Cross of Binding

1 AJS BEGINNING MAGICIAN WHEEL SUN	2 BKT CONNECTING H. PRIESTESS JUSTICE JUDGEMENT	3 CLU CREATING EMPRESS HANGED MAN WORLD
4 DMV BUILDING EMPEROR DEATH	5 ENW CHANGING HIEROPHANT TEMPERANCE	6 FOX UNITING LOVERS DEVIL
7 GPY DEFEATING CHARIOT TOWER	8 HQZ MOVING STRENGTH STAR	9 IR COMPLETING HERMIT MOON

Figure 23 - The Cross of Binding within The Vitruvian Square

The Cross of Binding (Figure 23) is created with all the odd

numbered locations in *The Vitruvian Square*: 1, 3, 5, 7, and 9. This specific

combination of numbers and locations not only represents someone who

is unbreakable, but an individual who finds his or her situation

inescapable and mandatory. This convergence of potential reflects

feelings of confinement, being held fast, or being impelled. This is more than the "boxed-in" beliefs that accompany the number 4. This formation brings with it a major driving force that causes the person being read to act out with all their instincts. They are driven by profound and sudden desires.

The following Tarot Major Arcana comprise the Cross of Binding: The Magician (I), The Wheel of Fortune (X), The Sun (XIX), The Empress (III), The Hanged Man (XII), The World (XXI), The Hierophant (V), Temperance (XIV), The Chariot (VII), The Tower (XVI), The Hermit (IX), and The Moon (XVII).

The various numbers, letters, meanings and Tarot cards speak of commitments, burdens, and compulsion. This may also be about the consequences of choices and decisions. Don't confuse this necessarily with pain and distress. Rather, this formation is more about being chained and constrained to a destiny that might, in fact, have been foreseen or taken into account earlier.

The complete lack of any of these squares indicates someone who is unusually easy going and has a laissez-faire attitude. In other words, the absence of all of these numbers means the individual is uninvolved and perhaps too soft.

For both the Desire and Binding patterns, you will notice that they "cross the heart" of *The Vitruvian Square*. You will remember from your childhood uttering the oath, "Cross my heart, and hope to die. Stick a needle in my eye." Just as the phrase "cross my heart" is meant as a commitment to keeping a promise so, too, do the Crosses of Desire and Binding indicate that there are practices and beliefs in a person's life that are steadfastly fixed in place.

These various geometric shapes and patterns demonstrate the additional layers of meaning and insight that are possible with *The Vitruvian Square*. They also show the flexibility you have as a reader in using the matrix. There are two more very interesting patterns that can be found within *The Vitruvian Square*; both based on the Kabbalah and its Tree of Life. I have saved that discussion for Part Fourteen.

PART EIGHT
CHOOSING THE SQUARES TO USE – THE BASICS

. . . for such an intellect nothing would be uncertain

and the future just like the past would be present before its eyes.

- Marquis de Laplace

The Vitruvian Square affords a number of primary techniques for selecting

the Places of Power you will use in a reading. These methods include the

use of names, dates, numbers, and cards. A classic numerology

framework arrays the standard alphabet against the number 1 through 9

(Figure 24).

1	2	3	4	5	6	7	8	9
A	B	C	D	E	F	G	H	I
J	K	L	M	N	O	P	Q	R
S	T	U	V	W	X	Y	Z	

Figure 24 - Classic Numerology Table

The Vitruvian Square draws on this classic correspondence but converts this tabulation to a 3x3 structure. The associations are maintained and the new layout offers greater opportunities for meaning that come from alchemy, Tarot, and colors.

The Name Method

Take a person's name. You may use just the first name, the first and last names, or the first, middle and last names depending on your preference. For each letter, place a circle in the corresponding location on *The Vitruvian Square*. If there are letters that arise for the same square more than once, put in multiple circles.

For an example, let's use the fictitious name: "RICHARD

DRACO." Plotting each of the letters of that name with a circle in the

appropriate squares, our chart looks like this (Figure 25):

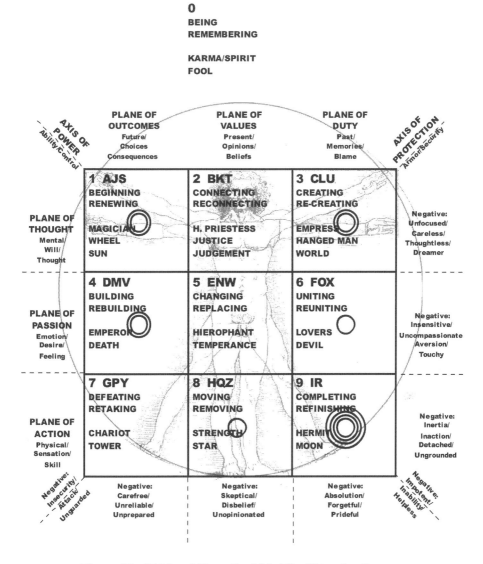

Figure 25 - "Richard Draco" within The Vitruvian Square

Even briefly glancing at the completed square and looking for the basic elements that have already been described in the book, you immediately see that all the numbers along the Plane of Duty are marked. Further, the square with the most marks is number 9. Both the Plane of Passion and the Axis of Protection would be complete if square number 5 was marked – but it is not. Finally, the Plane of Outcomes would be involved if square number 7 was marked – but it, too, is not in play. Thus, a reading for Mr. Draco might start like this:

[COMMENT: Using the Plane of Duty] You are someone who tends to focus on the past. In other words, you spend a lot of time concentrating on finding out who or what is responsible for things happening. Likewise, you are acutely aware of painful situations that might have brought you or threatened to convey dishonor on you – that is something you want to avoid at all costs.

[COMMENT: Using square 9 attributes] Now this all makes sense because you are someone who is in a constant state of completing things – you like things done and concluded. You don't like to leave things pending. You would rather finish and move on. And when you move on – boy, do you move on! You will readily wash your hands of a former, completed project and move your energy and focus to the next piece of work you believe awaits you. Sometimes this has caused others to think you are too detached or unaffectionate. In reality, you love the solitude that moving away and starting fresh bring you. You like being able to say, "I've done that" rather than saying, "I'm in the process of doing that now."

[COMMENT: Using the lack of square 5 attributes] It is interesting to see that, while you love to advance on to new projects and adventures, you must admit that you feel inside that you sometimes lack the power to bring your dreams to life. This happens to you when you fail to replace the old journey with a sense of direction and purpose. "Moving on" for the mere sake of "moving on" does not serve you well. When you start trusting your own wisdom, not only will your control over your life path improve but . . . [COMMENT: now focusing on the Plane of Passion] . . . you will discover your emotional center, as well. Once you find that passionate essence, you will discover a new flow of feelings that fuel your everyday endeavors.

[COMMENT: Using the lack of square 7 attributes]

Perhaps you would be best served for the moment to turn your attention to the future and to things you want to accomplish. This seems to be a more productive and fulfilling route for you rather than living in the past, don't you agree? In fact, instead of imagining all the things in the past that lead you to where you are now, starting visualizing how your choices and your conscious decisions will guide you to where you want to be.

While the foregoing is not a full reading, obviously, you can now see the wealth of information you have available to provide a reading for someone.

The Date Method

You can use a birth date, the current year, or any combination thereof, or an important event/occurrence date to lead you through a reading with *The Vitruvian Square*. Simply plug in the applicable date numbers in their corresponding squares similar to the way in which we handled letters. Thus, using a fictitious birthday of January 14, 1964, *The Vitruvian Square* would look like this (Figure 26):

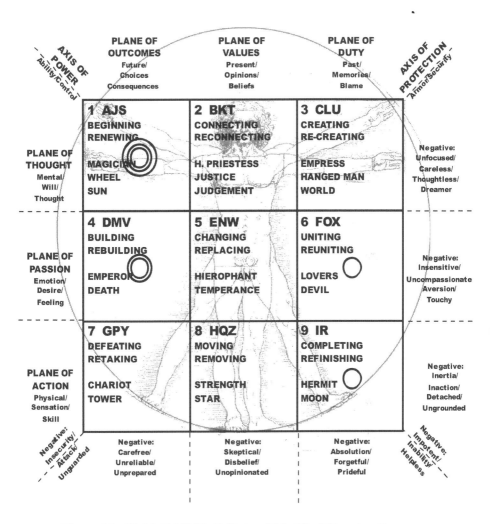

0
BEING
REMEMBERING

KARMA/SPIRIT
FOOL

AXIS OF POWER
Ability/Control

AXIS OF PROTECTION
Armor/Security

PLANE OF OUTCOMES Future/ Choices Consequences	PLANE OF VALUES Present/ Opinions/ Beliefs	PLANE OF DUTY Past/ Memories/ Blame

PLANE OF THOUGHT Mental/ Will/ Thought	**1 AJS** BEGINNING RENEWING MAGICIAN WHEEL SUN	**2 BKT** CONNECTING RECONNECTING H. PRIESTESS JUSTICE JUDGEMENT	**3 CLU** CREATING RE-CREATING EMPRESS HANGED MAN WORLD	Negative: Unfocused/ Careless/ Thoughtless/ Dreamer
PLANE OF PASSION Emotion/ Desire/ Feeling	**4 DMV** BUILDING REBUILDING EMPEROR DEATH	**5 ENW** CHANGING REPLACING HIEROPHANT TEMPERANCE	**6 FOX** UNITING REUNITING LOVERS DEVIL	Negative: Insensitive/ Uncompassionate Aversion/ Touchy
PLANE OF ACTION Physical/ Sensation/ Skill	**7 GPY** DEFEATING RETAKING CHARIOT TOWER	**8 HQZ** MOVING REMOVING STRENGTH STAR	**9 IR** COMPLETING REFINISHING HERMIT MOON	Negative: Inertia/ Inaction/ Detached/ Ungrounded

Negative:
Insecurity/
Attack/
Unguarded

Negative: Carefree/ Unreliable/ Unprepared	Negative: Skeptical/ Disbelief/ Unopinionated	Negative: Absolution/ Forgetful/ Prideful

Negative:
Impotent/
Inability/
Helpless

Figure 26 - "1-14-1964" Birth Date within The Vitruvian Square

Using just this birth date, we see that beginnings are extremely important to this person (square 1). There is a complete lack of attention to the Present and its corresponding Plane of Values (squares 2, 5, and 8). Likewise, there is a lack of the Axis of Protection (squares 3, 5, and 7). Thus, a reading for our Capricorn might start like this:

[COMMENT: Using square 1] Fresh starts and new beginnings are very important for you. So is control and being in charge of the creating. Not one to sit around and wait for things to happen to you, you use all of your mental energies to push past boredom, procrastination, and even rest. All of this creativity is tremendous, but don't forget that the pauses in life are as important as all your "goings and doings." There are times – and you already know this – when you need to pay attention to balance and give yourself a break.

[COMMENT: Using the missing square 5] The fact that you are such a control freak makes sense since you also move away from the concept of change. You so like things going your way and consistent with your expectations, you sometimes overlook that change is the spice of life. Indeed – take a deep breath now because I'm going to be using the "R" word – if you will just take a few more risks and allow yourself and your world a little more variety, you may find a whole new power available to you. Not only will your creative juices find faster materialization, your emotions and passion will expand exponentially.

[COMMENT: Using the square 4 attributes] When you do bring your passion and your desires together, you are an unstoppable force of nature. It's as if your intense wants make magic all on their own. You know that's not entirely true, however, and that your own personal faith and foundation are what give you the building blocks to make something empowering out of apparently nothing. At least that's how others see you.

[COMMENT: The lack of an Axis of Protection] Just as you hold yourself accountable for what happens around you, you also hold others responsible for their own lives. It is not that you don't care. Rather, you believe everything happens to people as a result of their own decisions and choices. While you are a marvelous guardian – when you feel it appropriate – most of the time you don't believe people are victims. As such, you spend little of your precious time shielding other people.

Interestingly, there is also an imposter complex about you. Other people will tell you that you are quite accomplished and quite capable of handling nearly everything. Deep down inside, however, you keep having to harness the demon that whispers: "You aren't good enough."

[COMMENT: Comparing the Planes of Outcomes and Values] Finally, you have an interesting dynamic going on with you. You seem to operate best when you are result oriented and outcomes focused. This "future" is where your creativity truly blossoms and you can form a solid palace of fortified beliefs and results. However, you don't like risk and confrontation and conflict, and this keeps you from living out your dreams as easily and quickly as you'd like.

Moreover, you have a tendency to relive the past – and your creativity seems to spring from that leaning. Simply put, it is when you "take charge" that you are future oriented, and when you "sit back and let things happen" you feel drawn to the past. You can have either or both – but I sense you are best served by moving forward rather than reliving what has been and is past.

The use of names and birth or event dates is just a start, however, since these types of indicators are admittedly stagnant, fixed, and necessarily do not change from reading to reading. Therefore, always add variety to the reading experiences by also including the current year or timing. In fact, combine names and dates together into one powerful, diverse chart reading.

You can use widely known and accepted numerology calculations with *The Vitruvian Square*. Here is a brief summary of some of those other methods; ways of arriving at the various Places of Power so that you will have enough variety to give readings to the same person more than once.

YOUR RULING/LIFE LESSON NUMBER: Take the full birth date and reduce it to one number. For example, March 15, 1964 (03/15/1964) ultimately reduces down to the number 2, as follows: 3 + 15 + 1964 = 3 + 6 (1 + 5) + 20 (1 + 9 + 6 + 4) = 29 = 11 (2 + 9) = 2 (1 + 1).

This number represents the lessons you must learn in this lifetime or those characteristics which are constant and cannot be changed. This number can also represent your vocation or the cosmic gift you are given in order to accomplish your destiny.

In our example, 2 (e.g., the matrix square of connecting and "The High Priestess") serves as the primary identifier. If we also look at the first total reached that is less than 21 (the highest Tarot card number) we have 11. Number 11 (e.g., the matrix square of reconnecting and "Justice" – remember the "re-" explanation I provided earlier) would be one of the supplements and characteristics that improves or shapes the qualities of the 2. 29 is not used because, as noted, there are only twenty-two Tarot Major Arcana and, even then, they only use numbers 0 through 21. The number 2 can also be thought of as 02 if you'd like. In that instance, the number 0 would be read as having a karmic overlay and Fate also has its finger in the lessons of this reading.

PERSONAL YEAR NUMBER: Take both the birth month and birth day numbers and add them to the year of the last birthday. For example, to obtain a personal year number for a birth date of March 7, 1958 (03/7/1958), you would use 3 (month) + 7 (day) + 2020 (this current year). This ultimately reduces down to the number 5, as follows:

$$3 + 7 + 2020 = 3 + 7 + 4 (2 + 0 + 2 + 0) = 14 = 5 (1 + 4).$$

This number represents the trend for the coming year.

The number 5 represents change and uncertainty and the ruling aspects of The Hierophant. The supporting 14 presents itself as replacing and Temperance (or, in other words, a move in a new direction, the resetting of what was once a normal way of doing things, and the need for balance and patience in unsure times). As before, you can add the 0's and discuss the play of Fate and Destiny.

SOUL NUMBER: This is arrived at by adding together the numerical equivalents of only the vowels in someone's name. If you can't remember these correspondences, take a look back at Part Three. For example, if we are working with someone named "Alfred Garland" that name ultimately reduces down to the number 8, as follows: each "A" equates to 1 and the "E" equates to 5. So, ALFRED GARLAND would be broken down as A + E + A + A = 1 + 5 + 1 + 1 = 8.

This number represents what one truly desires to be and what the inner self seeks. This is a person's real personality and the accumulated growth from prior lives.

In our example, 8 would represent, among other things, moving (changing location) and The Hermit. As such, a number 8 soul number is someone who needs to stay in motion as well as someone who relishes solitude.

I hasten to add that I treat the letter "Y" as a vowel. So, for example, the name "Bryan" would have the vowels "Y" and "A" present.

OUTER PERSONALITY NUMBER: Add together the numerical equivalents of only the consonants in someone's name. Continuing with our last example, the name "Alfred Garland" ultimately reduces down to the number 5, as follows: ALFRED GARLAND would be L + F + R + D + G + R + L + N + D = 3 + 6 + 9 + 4 + 7 + 9 + 3 + 5 + 4 = 50 = 5 (5 + 0).

This number represents how you appear to others and what others expect from you.

With our example, the number 5 would be read as an individual who not only handles change and transformation well, but someone who is able to relay wisdom to the general public (rather than dealing with an enlightened few).

PATH OF DESTINY NUMBER: Add together the numerical equivalents of each letter of the entire name. For example, the name "Alfred Garland" ultimately reduces down to the number 4, as follows: 1 (A) + 3 (L) + 6 (F) + 9 (R) + 5 (E) + 4 (D) + 7 (G) + 1 (A) + 9 (R) + 3 (L) + 1 (A) + 5 (N) + 4 (D) = 58 = 13 (5 + 8) = 4.

This number represents what a person must do in this lifetime or what they came here to manifest. This is the path you must walk.

In this example, you will use the number 4 as the primary, base number. This is someone who must build and establish, supervise, and rule. This is The Emperor who commands. You will also use the number 13 as a supporting number which provides you the additional insight that this is a person who not only fleshes out the abstract, but someone who can put things back together again when necessary.

PART NINE
CHOOSING THE SQUARES TO USE – THE THREEFOLD NUMBER METHOD

The present is theirs;

the future, for which I have really worked, is mine.

- Nikola Tesla

This is by far the method I find most rewarding for selecting Places of Power to read from *The Vitruvian Square*. It is always one of the techniques I employ when doing a live show, media appearance, or performance for a group of people. It is a descendant of older techniques from Walter Gorn Old and Sydney Omarr.

Dr. Walter Gorn Old was an English mystic and astrologer who used the penname "Sepharial" in the late 19ᵗʰ and early 20ᵗʰ centuries. In his delightfully sizeable treatise, "The Kabala of Numbers," Sepharial first suggested selecting nine random numbers, arriving at a total, and then adding 3 to that sum. Following in his footsteps, Omarr adjusted the Sepharial system and primarily advised the use of just three numbers added together.

Omarr exhorted readers to decide on the chosen numbers by using his "Thought Dial" wheel (a wheel printed on cardboard with a spinning dial attached and which allowed you to choose from the numbers 1 through 9, 11, and 22). Omarr called his process a "valid, mantic procedure for tapping the subconscious." Literally swallowed up in a passage later in his booklet, Omarr mentions merely jotting down three numbers when the wheel is not available. Revisiting both Sepharial and Omarr for use with *The Vitruvian Square*, I discovered a wonderful, unerring process that is so simple you might, in fact, be inclined to dismiss it.

I urge you to set aside such thoughts and give this a try!

The threefold number technique is simply this: name any three numbers that pop into your head while thinking of the person you are reading or question you are contemplating. Now add these numbers together. There is no need to limit the range of numbers from which you choose. ANY THREE NUMBERS WILL WORK. And . . . duplicate numbers may be selected. The important part is to allow the numbers to surface freely from your subconscious. Do not give the choice of numbers too much premeditation or thought. Just allow the numbers to appear for you in your inner vision as you think upon a person or event or topic.

For example, let's say I am giving a reading and the numbers that come to mind are: 27, 12, and 36. Added together, those three numbers give me the sum of 75 (27 + 12 + 36). Reducing down the 75, 7 + 5 results in the number 12. Now reduce the 12 and you ultimately stop at 3 (1 + 2). I will remember the 12, however, and use that for a deeper, more layered part of the reading. In fact, in some cases, I will even use the sums of the three original numbers to add more detail to the reading. So, in this case I would be using 9 (2 + 7), 3 (1 + 2), and 9 (3 + 6). The conversation then proceeds:

[COMMENT: Using square 3 first] You are in a creating frame of mind right now and you have a current need to bring something into existence. Moreover, you, yourself, are in a state of "becoming." [COMMENT: Now moving to The Empress aspect of the square, I can tell a large portion of what you are doing at the moment is creating through being receptive and approachable. You are ready and willing to encounter new ideas, inspiration and input openly. [COMMENT: Using the combined Medicine Wheel and Minor Arcana aspects (techniques that I describe a little later)] I am also drawn to the East. This tells me your judgment, perceptions, and opinions are primarily at work in your creative process. I also sense that the color "yellow" figures prominently for you right now. In other words, I sense great happiness and joy around you. Still, there is some caution or forethought that is keeping you from fully realizing your potential. [COMMENT: Using the number 12] At a deeper level, the particular creativity phase you are experiencing also involves your need to connect with yourself, your ideas, and others. You are as much reaching out as you are reaching within. [COMMENT: Using the two number 9's and number 3] Finally, all of this innovation and artistry you are seeking is a means for you to restore yourself – kind of a start-over for you. Once this new "you" occurs, you are best served by keeping your new-found visions to yourself for a while. Savor them and become intimate with them before sharing with others.

You will notice that I recommend you – the one giving the reading – selecting the three numbers rather than having the person receiving the reading making the selection. While you can certainly have someone else provide the numbers, I personally find that you obtain more precision when the sum comes from you because of your intimacy with *The Vitruvian Square* and your understanding of what is happening. That being said, there will be times when it is more beneficial to have the other person select the numbers to be used because it compels the individual to instantly be involved in the reading. I save this approach for those situations when I need to overcome the negativity of a "doubting Thomas."

PART TEN
CHOOSING THE SQUARES TO USE – FURTHER ADVENTURES

One day Alice came to a fork in the road

and saw a Cheshire cat in a tree.

Which road to take? she asked.

Where do you want to go? was his response.

I don't know, Alice answered.

Then, said, the cat, it doesn't matter.

- Lewis Carroll

In Part Eight on number selection, you were provided with a basic groundwork for generating the Places of Power within *The Vitruvian Square* to use for a reading. While these essentials are a terrific way to

start your reading and provide you with a baseline of what has led up to
an individual's Present, you can quickly see how the formulas bestow an
unchanging arrangement. Your birth date does not change. Similarly,
your formal, given name does not change (although you might use
variations of it in everyday life). You want to be able to present new
"readings" and cutting-edge studies of people.

The Threefold Number Method (from Part Nine) certainly
provides you with a nearly limitless range of numbers so that your
readings remain fresh and you aren't simply repeating yourself time and
time again. For those occasions when you want even more variation and
the use of some groundbreaking rituals, you will enjoy what follows. I am
giving you the descriptions based on the use of a set of cards (whether
those are Tarot, Lenormand, or some other oracle cards). Naturally, you
can convert these descriptions for use with any other type of oracular
device you prefer.

The Play of Readings

One more way to use *The Vitruvian Square* for a reading is to do
what I call the "Readings of Readings." Simply, each Place of Power
within *The Vitruvian Square* is a mini-reading. Whether you use Tarot

cards, Lenormand cards, or other oracle cards like *The Deck of Shadows* –

the oracle deck that I created – you will lay out nine cards and then

determine, based on input from your sitter, which of the squares to use.

Each particular Place of Power has a designated theme that you then use

for a reading.

Here are the Places of Power and their corresponding reading:

SQUARE 1: Feel Free to move what is stuck.

SQUARE 2: Feel free to disguise what is exposed.

SQUARE 3: Feel free to tame what is wild.

SQUARE 4: Feel free to command what is unruly.

SQUARE 5: Feel free to open what is closed.

SQUARE 6: Feel free to know what is unexplored.

SQUARE 7: Feel free to destroy what is built.

SQUARE 8: Feel free to bear what is loose.

SQUARE 9: Feel free to end what is started.

1 FEEL FREE TO MOVE WHAT IS STUCK	2 FEEL FREE TO DISGUISE WHAT IS EXPOSED	3 FEEL FREE TO TAME WHAT IS WILD
4 FEEL FREE TO COMMAND WHAT IS UNRULY	5 FEEL FREE TO OPEN WHAT IS CLOSED	6 FEEL FREE TO KNOW WHAT IS UNEXPLORED
7 FEEL FREE TO DESTROY WHAT IS BUILT	8 FEEL FREE TO BEAR WHAT IS LOOSE	9 FEEL FREE TO END WHAT IS STARTED

Figure 27 - The Play of Readings

Here are the steps to the Readings of Readings layout:

STEP 1: Shuffle and cut the cards.

STEP 2: Place nine cards face down using *The Vitruvian Square* matrix - a 3x3 matrix.

STEP 3: Tell your sitter what each of the Places of Power means using the correspondences, above.

STEP 4: Have your sitter tell you which of the "Feel free to . . ."

themes calls to them the most.

STEP 5: Turn over the card in that particular Place of Power and read that card in the context of the "Feel free to" theme.

STEP 6: Draw more cards, as needed, to do a deeper reading of that particular Place of Power focus.

The Play of Nearness

You can also do a straightforward ten card reading using *The Vitruvian Square* matrix to determine what is "about to happen", as follows:

STEP 1: Shuffle and cut the cards.

STEP 2: Place ten cards face down using *The Vitruvian Square* matrix - a 3x3 matrix with one card at the top in the 0 position. You deal the 0 card position first, then the 1 card position, and so forth all the way through the 9 card position.

STEP 3: You read only these ten cards, as follows:

SQUARE 0: This is the door that is about to open/close.

SQUARE 1: This is what is about to appear.

SQUARE 2: This is the puzzle that is about to be solved.

SQUARE 3: This is what is about to refuse to leave.

SQUARE 4: This is the rule you are about to follow.

SQUARE 5: This is the hole (whole) you are about to fall in.

SQUARE 6: This is the restriction that is about to bend.

SQUARE 7: This is what you are about to change.

SQUARE 8: This is what is about to rise.

SQUARE 9: This is what is about to vanish.

0
THIS IS THE
DOOR THAT IS
ABOUT TO
OPEN/CLOSE

1 **THIS IS** **WHAT IS** **ABOUT TO** **APPEAR**	**2** **THIS IS THE** **PUZZLE THAT** **IS ABOUT TO** **BE SOLVED**	**3** **THIS IS** **WHAT IS** **ABOUT TO** **REFUSE TO** **LEAVE.**
4 **THIS IS THE** **RULE YOU** **ARE ABOUT** **TO FOLLOW**	**5** **THIS IS THE** **HOLE** **(WHOLE) YOU** **ARE ABOUT** **TO FALL IN**	**6** **THIS IS THE** **RESTRICT-** **ION THAT IS** **ABOUT TO** **BEND**
7 **THIS IS** **WHAT YOU** **ARE** **ABOUT TO** **CHANGE**	**8** **THIS IS** **WHAT IS** **ABOUT TO** **RISE**	**9** **THIS IS WHAT** **IS ABOUT TO** **VANISH**

Figure 28 - The Play of Nearness

The Deck of Shadows, Tarot, and Playing Cards

We previously explored deciding upon numbers through the use of standard numerological formulas and seemingly chance figures that come to your mind. I happen to use *The Deck of Shadows* when I want to deepen the divinatory experience. By using an object – in this case a deck of oracle cards – to further the reading, you change the focus of the session from the signs and symbols you are internally receiving to what the "cards" are telling you about the person who is receiving the reading. This is not a trivial distinction to be ignored. Quite the contrary. There are times when it does not matter where the intuitive guidance comes from. There are other situations, however, where mythic accoutrements intensify the participation in and believability of the undertaking.

You don't have to use *The Deck of Shadows* for the steps I am about to describe. You may use a regular deck of playing cards or even a Tarot deck. Indeed, you are merely looking for cards that have numbers on them.

Previously, I used the name, "RICHARD DRACO," to show you how the letters of that name unfold into various Places of Power within *The Vitruvian Square*. The name, itself, is not going to change from one moment to the next. Therefore, you will use the letters that make up "RICHARD DRACO" to tell you what the individual has brought with him to the reading – essentially the vibrations, opportunities, and traits with which "RICHARD DRACO" was born. Now you are going to be able to read what he has done with those attributes and qualities.

Take a deck of cards. Shuffle and cut them and spread them out face down before you. Now select one card for each letter of the chosen name – in this example you will choose 12 cards; one for each letter of "RICHARD DRACO's" name. You are not using *The Vitruvian Square* matrix, yet. Right now, you're simply dealing out cards to match the letters of the name.

Let's presume you have selected the following cards from *The Deck of Shadows:* Ace of Clubs (Knowledge), 7 of Diamonds (Maturation), 7 of Hearts (Visions), Jack of Hearts (Dreams), Kings of Hearts (The Void), Queen of Clubs (Transformation), 4 of Spades (Resurrection), 7 of Spades (Revenge), 3 of Diamonds (Triumph), 9 of Hearts (Riddle), 9 of Diamonds (Wretched Excess), and 6 of Clubs (Freedom).

Aces are considered 1, Jacks are 11, and reduced down to 2 (1 +

1), Queens are 12 and reduced down to 3 (1 + 2), and Kings are 13 and

reduced down to 4 (1 + 3). Thus, we have the following numbers to fill into *The Vitruvian Square*: 1-7-7-2-4-3-4-7-3-9-9-6. Now, we're going to

fill in *The Vitruvian Square* with the numbers we just obtained. Using *The*

Vitruvian Square, the squares would now be marked (Figure 29):

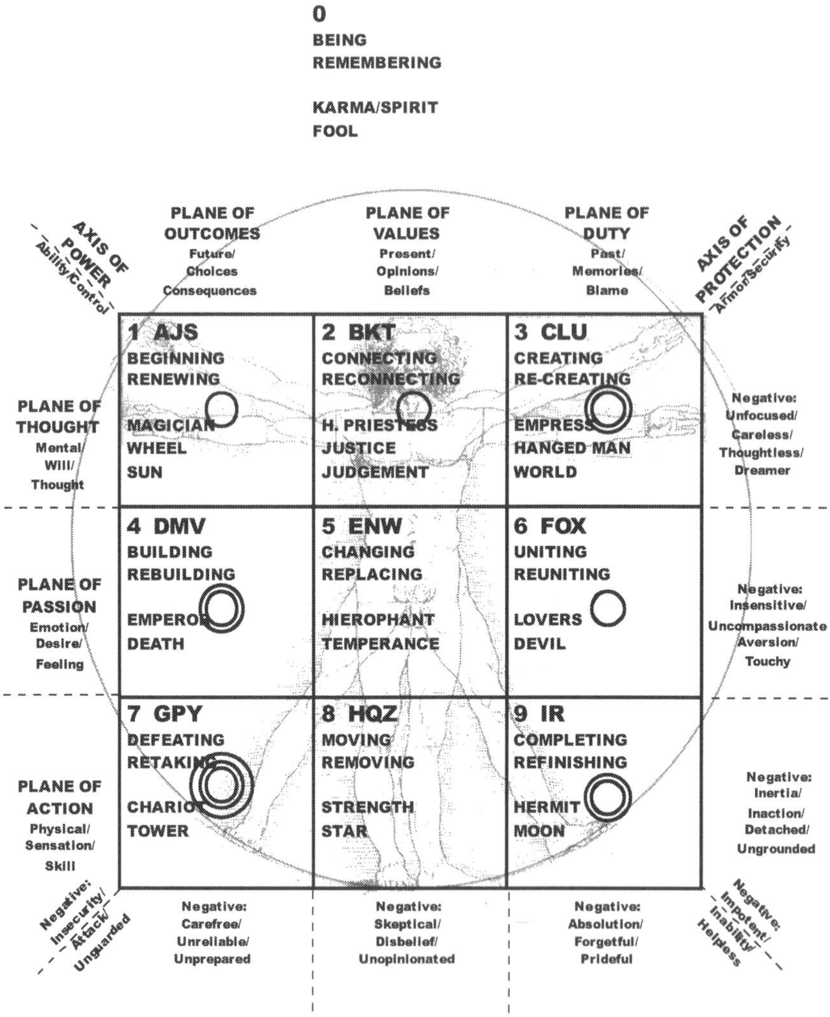

Figure 29 - Cards Used with The Name "Richard Draco" within
The Vitruvian Square

Comparing our "new" numbers with the ones initially used for "RICHARD DRACO's" name, we see that the number 5 is still missing. The Plane of Duty (squares 3, 6, and 9) still exists. Now, however, we also have the Planes of Outcomes (squares 1, 4, and 7) and Thought (squares 1, 2, and 3) at play. You should also note that with the original reading using the name, square 9 was the main element. In this current reading, square 7 now commands.

Thus, a new short reading for Mr. Draco would be:

[COMMENT: Using the missing 5] Interestingly, you still have not learned to fully communicate your dreams and desires to the outside world. They might be clear to you internally and to a select few, but they need greater expression. [COMMENT: Using the Plane of Thoughts] It is not enough for you to merely think about your needs and wants. You are truly looking to manifest your visions – something that is going to require even more mental discipline over the challenges of your material world. [COMMENT: Using the 7 and 9, and the missing 8] I do sense that you are ready to start breaking through and taking charge of your life. Previously, you will recall, I noted that you were essentially focused on a rebirth or start-over. Now, you just want to make things happen! For that to occur, you need to show some self-restraint and control.

[COMMENT: Using the Plane of Outcomes] Most importantly for you is the change in your center of attention. Where once you were concerned with the blame and shame and causation of the Past, you are now looking to the Future. This will serve you well since the time ahead is the fertile ground for your creativity and plans.

For those of you who wish to use *The Deck of Shadows* or Tarot cards to enhance the reading, pay particular attention to the patterns in which the cards, themselves, fall. In our example using *The Deck of Shadows*, we have the 7 square inhabited by the themes "Maturation," "Visions," and "Revenge." We also have the 9 square inhabited by "Riddle" and "Wretched Excess." It is easy to see how a discussion of "Triumph" (7) can be enriched with an explanation of how paying attention to wise and responsible aspirations will finally allow this individual to overcome the recriminations of the Past. Likewise, we can explain how the theme of "Achievement" (9) is accentuated by the message that curiosity can likely lead to intemperance and self-indulgence and that undue curiosity should be a warning.

The analysis and use would be no different if you are working with Tarot cards, instead. Simply select the particular number of Tarot cards you wish to use for the reading and then lay them out according to their numerical equivalents. In the case of Tarot cards (as opposed to *The Deck of Shadows* or regular playing cards):

Pages are the eleventh card in a particular suit so they equate to 2 (11 or 1 + 1)

Knights are the twelfth card in a particular suit so they equate to 3 (12 or 1 + 2)

Queens are the thirteenth card in a particular suite so they equate to 4 (13 or 1 + 3)

Kings are the fourteenth card in a particular suit so they equate to 5 (14 or 1 + 4)

The Platonic Solids

If you have ever seen Role-Playing Game ("RPG") dice, you already know about Platonic Solids. Named after Plato, these are dice with 4, 6, 8, 12, and 20 faces (Figure 30). Plato speculated that the elements – Earth, Air, Fire and Water – were all built from these solid shapes.

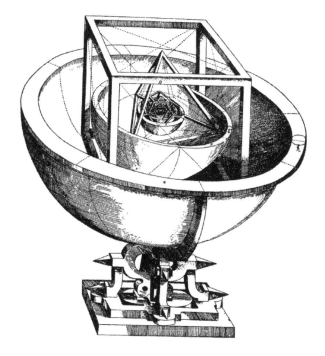

Figure 30 - Johannes Kepler's Platonic Solid Model of The Universe (1596)

The Platonic Solids in their incarnation as dice have been discussed for ages. In fact, it appears that the various shapes for dice are consistent with the discovery and representations of the Platonic Solids.

When I speak of Sacred Geometry I am referring to those patterns that exist within the various dimensions. It was understood by the Ancients that people studying and grasping this previously concealed order and fundamental design of the Universe would gain wisdom of the workings of venerable mysteries. Sacred Geometry not only exists spontaneously in nature but it is intentionally used in architecture, art, music, and . . . the Platonic Solids.

I am going to use these concepts with *The Vitruvian Square* to provide you a fun, unbelievably visual, and unconventional means of obtaining numbers and Places of Power for our readings. Simply, visit any hobby or gaming store (or order online) and obtain what are referred to as RPG dice. These are six multi-sided dice (the five Platonic Solids – 4-sided, 6-sided, 8-sided, 10-sided, 12-sided, 20-sided dice – and one 10-sided percentile die which we will not be using for this discussion). RPG dice have numbers on them. For this discussion, we're only interested in examining how to use the die's shapes for a reading. In that regard, the Platonic Solids dice provide you the ability to add specific elemental designators to a reading depending on which ones are selected and in what order they are chosen.

To begin, show the six dice and have the person for whom you are providing a reading place them in order from their most preferred to their least preferred. The direction of the row of dice does not matter so long as you know which is the best liked and which is the least liked. This will automatically provide you with information on where the emphasis on your reading should be. For example, let's suppose the dice are chosen in this order: 8-sided, 6-sided, 10-sided, 4-sided, 20-sided, and 12-

sided. Among other things, I now know this individual is very focused on their thinking and new ideas at the moment. At the same time, I know they are not giving enough attention to their feelings and emotions.

Using the attributes outlined below, you will make a quick assessment of the person selecting the dice. Remember, you are focusing on the dice shapes – not the numbers they might have imprinted on them.

Now I want you imagine a large version of *The Vitruvian Square* is projected onto the tabletop or casting surface between you and the person being read. It is oriented so that the top (1, 2, and 3) is farthest from you and the bottom (7, 8, and 9) is closest to you.

Although you can certainly use an actual cloth or mat with *The Vitruvian Square* drawn or printed on it, for this exercise let's start learning to project our imagination on a location. Take a moment right now and look in front of you at some surface. Start practicing being able to visualize *The Vitruvian Square* projected onto it. This skill will be especially useful a little later when I speak about palmistry.

Once this imaginary *Vitruvian Square* is fixed in your mind's eye, have the dice cast onto the reading surface. Notice where the dice fall within the imaginary basic layout. Notice which die falls where and if there are other dice nearby. Just as with any other Sortilege or Cleromancy methods (also called the casting of lots to divine the Future and explain the Past and Present), notice the patterns that the dice make together after they arrive at the final resting places. In other words, notice all the things you would ordinarily observe if there was actually a *Vitruvian Square* printed on the throwing surface.

If you want to start using this particular casting/reading technique right away and don't have ready access to RPG dice, you can also use coins, stones, crystals, and runes with your *Vitruvian Square* reading. Any and all such items may be cast upon your imaginary layout. As I just indicated, pay attention to the patterns that are now formed on your imaginary *Vitruvian Square*.

In reading the objects that have been cast, here are the patterns I generally see and use:

1. Items that form a Triangle mean good fortune attached to the Places of Power that the Triangle touches.

2. Items that form a Square show the need for attention and prudence for those areas represented by the involved Places of Power.

3. Items that form a Circle indicate triumph and abundance for the Place of Power covered by the Circle.

4. Items that form a Cross evidence a blockage or obstruction for the involved locations.

Of course, there are many more symbols and shapes that will be formed as you gain experience with this method of using *The Vitruvian Square*. Once you identify a symbol that has been cast, ask yourself what that symbol means for you, personally. Your own personal identification with the shape and the subtext you bring to that association are the most important clues you can have for giving your reading. In other words, you will be relying on your own personal connections to the patterns and shapes that are disclosed.

There may also be times when the casting will reveal a letter. Pay particular attention to the letter that has formed as this will likely refer to a person who will play a major part in the subject of the reading.

Now that I have shown you how to do castings with *The Vitruvian Square*, let's return to the selection of particular dice shapes. In using the Platonic Solids, have the person who is receiving the reading look at the various dice and select the one that calls out to be chosen. The choice of the die means:

4-Sided

Figure 31 - 4-Sided Die

The 4-sided die (Figure 31) represents the element "Fire" and contains the numbers 1 through 4. This is also the fourth state of matter known as "plasma." This state is distinct from a solid or a liquid and requires heating to exist. Someone who chooses this die is someone with an intense emotional makeup. He or she is easily aroused. The person receiving the reading usually provokes others to action and reaction. Moreover, this type of individual generally finds himself displaced or disturbed most of the time.

This die brings together the concepts of beginning (1), connecting (2), creating (3), and building (4).

6-Sided

Figure 32 - 6-Sided Die

The 6-sided die (Figure 32) is the die you are most familiar with and which is used in most board games. It usually contains only the numbers 1 through 6. This shape represents the element "Earth" and is one of the four elements thought to compose the Universe. When you think about it, it makes sense, then, that this die epitomizes that which is solid, firm, and hearty. The person choosing this die is down-to-earth, lively, and potentially lusty. This is someone who is also practical and sensible.

This die brings together the concepts of beginning (1), connecting (2), creating (3), building (4), changing (5), and uniting (6).

8-Sided

Figure 33 - 8-Sided Die

The 8-sided die (Figure 33) represents the element "Air" and usually contains the numbers 1 through 8. Air, too, is one of the four elements thought to form the Universe. After all, air is what we all need to breathe! Someone who chooses this die is open to new ideas and teeming with thoughts and enthusiasm. Be warned, however, that the person choosing the 8-sided die may also be impractical and highly speculative. In fact, this type of individual may be viewed by their friends, lovers, and associates as a visionary but someone who needs to be grounded.

This die brings together the concepts of beginning (1), connecting (2), creating (3), building (4), changing (5), uniting (6), defeating (7), and moving (8).

10-Sided

Figure 34 - 10-Sided Die

The 10-sided die (Figure 34) usually contains the numbers 1 through 10. It represents the ideas of "Fortune," "Fate," and "Chance." Someone who chooses this die loves abundance and generally knows how to chase Fate (if not outright capture and control it). In choosing this die, the person receiving the reading also believes in both Fate and Luck and is not afraid to take risks. Indeed, adventure is the name of the game here as it is invigorating and pregnant with possibilities.

This die brings together the concepts of beginning (1), connecting (2), creating (3), building (4), changing (5), uniting (6), defeating (7), moving (8), completing (9), and renewing (10).

12-Sided

Figure 35 - 12-Sided Die

The 12-sided die (Figure 35) usually contains the numbers 1 through 12 and represents "Water." Water is one of the four elements that make up the world around us. It is the ingredient absolutely necessary for the life of most living things. In fact, if you think of most expeditions around our planet and our search for life in outer space, one of the first things sought is water. Like the element, itself, the person who chooses this die may be all things to all people and has a personality that seeps into the tiniest crevice to explore, makes himself at home, and even pries open the most stubborn of people. You will find the person who makes this selection to be quite an emotional individual who may be "colorless" one moment and "frozen" the next.

This die brings together the concepts of beginning (1), connecting (2), creating (3), building (4), changing (5), uniting (6), defeating (7), moving (8), completing (9), renewing (10), reconnecting

(11), and recreating (12).

20-Sided

Figure 36 - 20-Sided Die

This last of our dice – the 20-sided die (Figure 36) – usually has the numbers 1 through 20 on it. The die represents the ideas of "The Universe" and of wholeness with everything. The Universe can exist in a vacuum. However, the selection of this die can also be an attempt by the person making the choice to have everything stated or known at all times. This type of individual wants quantity as much as he thrives quality. "The more the better," is often the slogan to be heard.

This die brings together the concepts of beginning (1), connecting (2), creating (3), building (4), changing (5), uniting (6), defeating (7), moving (8), completing (9), renewing (10 and 19), reconnecting (11 and 20), recreating (12), rebuilding (13), replacing (14), reuniting (15), retaking (16), removing (17), and refinishing (18).

You can also use each die in combination with another to generate random numbers. In doing so, you will add up the number shown on the top of each rolled die to arrive at a grand total. That total is then reduced down until you reach a smaller number that coincides with *The Vitruvian Square's* Places of Power. For example, if you roll all six dice and get 18 (20-sided die), 10 (12-sided die), 10 (10-sided die), 6 (8-sided die), 1 (6-sided die), and 3 (4-sided die), you get a grant total of 48 (18 + 10 + 10 + 6 + 1 + 3). 48 would then reduce down to 12 (4 + 8) which would, in turn, reduce down further to 3 (1 + 2). You would initially read *The Vitruvian Square* correspondences for the number 3 and then supplement that reading with the correspondences for the number 12.

Sacred Geometry

For some added depth to your readings, you will also want to be aware of the following associations of the various sacred geometrical shapes within *The Vitruvian Square* (Figure 37).

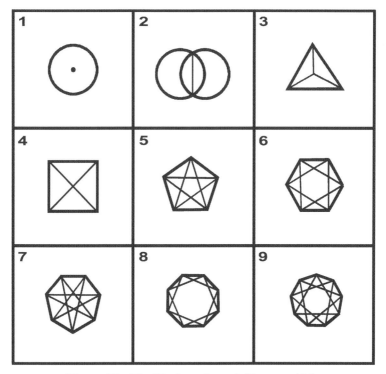

**Figure 37 - The Various Sacred Shapes within
The Vitruvian Square**

The first thing to do is simply "look" at the various basic shapes

and then notice the "designs within the designs" that arise. There is much

that can and has been written about Sacred Geometry. At the very least I

want you to know the following concepts/figures and apply them to your

readings.

Circle – Square 1

The simplest and most perfect of shapes, this is the ultimate expression of oneness. It is the Universe and the undivided whole.

Vesica Piscis – Square 2

Also called a "mandorla," here we have the symbol of mutual understanding represented by the coming together of two circles at their mid-points. The resulting shape in the center - commonly known as the *Vesica Piscis* – forms the shape of a human eye or a womb. As such, it is also thought of as the essence of the goddess energy. Because it also represents the joining together of the male and female energies, this symbol becomes the place from which everything is born. It is also the representation of what results from opposition.

Triangle – Square 3

With this shape, the Triangle, we have the three faces of existence. This represents resolved differences and the harmonizing of squares 1 and 2. This is one of those symbols that when rotated, has different meanings and emphasis. It can mean male or female depending on whether it is pointed up or down. When you get to the discussion of Alchemy, you will find that the triangle is also used to depict the four main elements that were once thought to make up existence.

Square – Square 4

The Square is another of the most basic shapes in nature, Sacred Geometry, and the Platonic Solids. It represents the existing state of affairs and the stability that comes from things and people being firm and steadfast. The Square represents someone who values situations that are static and free from change or variation. It is the Earth and a grounded personality. It also represents the four elements (Earth, Air, Fire, and Water) brought together as a cohesive whole.

Pentagon – Square 5

The Pentagon is the shape of the "Ideal" and of perfection. This shape gives birth to the pentagram - a star born within the figure. It represents not only transcendence but embodies life, itself, as it does or might exist in the holiest sense. The shape has far reaching effects as it represents the inclusion of Spirit combined in perfect balance with the four elements (Earth, Air, Fire, and Water). Essentially, this form adds the concept of bringing the spark of life into play.

Hexagon – Square 6

The six sides of this shape form the most stable figure with the most space. It represents, then, the concepts of form, utility, and function. This has also been called Nature's "perfect shape" and you will find this pattern naturally occurring in snowflakes and beehives.

Heptagon – Square 7

When the Triangle is added to the Square you get this shape. It represents the number of manifestation and results. The Ancients called the number 7 the virgin number. This is also illustrative of the seven ages of man and the colors of the rainbow. This shape serves as a bridge with all the other numbers and shapes. It is also a chasm - a deep opening - as it is the only number that does not fit precisely within a circle because of its irregular shape.

Octagon – Square 8

Not only can this shape be formed by combining two squares, it can also be formed by eight equilateral triangles. It is a labyrinth with the accompanying risk of getting lost. It is the shape that brings the reward of finding yourself. It can be thought of as the dance between Heaven and Earth. Indeed, many religious structures contain domes designed around an octagon.

Nonahedron – Square 9

This is the combination of three Triangles. It can be likened to the horizon - as you move closer, this number/figure/shape just seems to move away from you.

All of the discussion in this chapter is designed to provide you with a way of giving readings based on very ancient and sacred traditions. Many believe the shapes that make up the Platonic Solids and the various Sacred Geometry figures hold the keys that will unlock the secret patterns of our common lives and everyday experiences. You have now been provided with formulas for opening your readings to a whole new level.

In conclusion, *The Vitruvian Square* with Sacred Geometry applied would look like this (Figure 38):

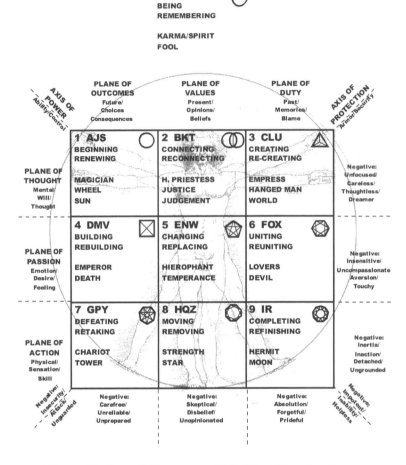

Figure 38 - Sacred Geometry within The Vitruvian Square

PART ELEVEN
MYTHIC READINGS WITH
THE VITRUVIAN SQUARE

The big question is whether you are going to be able

to say a hearty 'yes' to your adventure."

- Joseph Campbell

1 THE CALL TO ADVENTURE	2 REFUSAL OF THE CALL	3 SUPER- NATURAL AID
4 CROSSING THE THRESHOLD	5 BELLY OF THE WHALE	6 MEETING WITH THE GODDESS
7 THE ULTIMATE BOON	8 MASTER OF THE TWO WORLDS	9 FREEDOM TO LIVE

Figure 39 - The Monomyth within The Vitruvian Square

Myths effectively and elegantly explain how people experience life. Each of us is the hero in our own tale. In using *The Vitruvian Square* to provide legendary readings (Figure 39), you will be helping others to see the journey of Self they will start, are in the midst of, or have just completed. In other words, you will able to show others the legend and romance that is their own life story.

Myths are as much metaphorical as they are literal. Indeed, there are patterns that people follow that allow us to predict what the next stage of life will hold. While the order or arrangement of the specific mythic touchstones in each person's life may vary, the actual ingredients of each person's life remain nearly identical with others. As readers, we have only to determine the order that is being followed by a specific individual in order to provide insight into what has already happened, what is being experienced "now," and what is likely to be discovered and experienced in the future. In fact, by using *The Vitruvian Square* you will be able to give someone reasons and justifications for the events and decisions in their world and how those came to be. You will empower them through the next challenges they will encounter.

The Three Phases

The term "monomyth" was coined by Joseph Campbell and refers to the regularly repeated sequences we experience more commonly known as "The Hero's Journey" – an inner odyssey to self-awareness. It generally involves a hero going on an adventure and experiencing a very personal and powerful transformation. The sequences of the journey are initially divided into three main sections which directly correspond with *The Vitruvian Square's* three planes, as follows:

MONOMYTH	THE VITRUVIAN SQUARE
The Departure	Plane of Thought
The Initiation	Plane of Passion
The Return	Plane of Action

Both The Departure and Plane of Thought are concerned with a person's knowledge and understanding prior to setting out on the mythic journey. In a reading, then, when squares 1, 2, and 3 are all indicated (what you have previously learned as "The Plane of Thought"), you have someone who is "thinking" about or considering a quest, a change, a personal exploration, and the need to transform. When The Departure is present in a reading this indicates that there are further questions on the part of the person being read, curiosity that is at play, and plans to be made that are indicated. There is a desire to move away from the everyday world for something more exciting, if not better. These types of people need to be concerned with getting lost in their own thoughts and having their "head in the clouds."

Both The Initiation and Plane of Passion are concerned with a person's feelings, actions, and reactions while on the path of the mythic journey. When the squares 4, 5, and 6 are marked (what you have previously learned as "The Plane of Passion"), you are relating with someone who is actually in the course of their personal adventure and about to find or in the midst of finding a grand goal. When The Initiation is present in a reading, you have someone who wants to prove that they are worthy of hero status; that they can face the questions, the tasks, and the trials and be deserving of victory – both physically and spiritually. These type of people need to be concerned with being too emotional and wearing their "heart on their sleeves."

Both The Return and Plane of Action are concerned with a person's sophisticated and learned ways of doing things; knowledge gained from having started, gone through, and returned from the mythic journey. This is demonstrated by the presence of squares 7, 8, and 9 in a reading (what you previously learned as "The Plane of Action"). When all of these squares are present, you are face to face with someone who is street smart. They have a common sense born from adventure. When The Return is evident in a reading, this does not mean that the challenges have stopped. Quite the contrary. With The Return, you now have someone who is able to conquer life and take on challenges head-on. This is also someone who wants to share their knowledge and information with others. These types of people need to be concerned with being too earthbound, rigid, and being "stuck in one place."

As in all else with *The Vitruvian Square*, you are looking for identifiable and detectable patterns in your reading; essentially, the road that is being taken at the moment. In looking for this pathway, take into consideration whether the route is well formed or lacking definition, highly frequented or rarely visited, straight or winding. The essential quality of your hero's trail also provides you with items to speak about during the reading.

Stages of the Adventure

Now we move on to investigate the distinct stages or episodes that make up our mythic reading. Each one of these stages matches one of the Places of Power we have already reviewed. In a reading you will not only be using the following characteristics, you will continue to use the messages and interpretations considered earlier in the book. You are not ignoring one set of meanings for the other. Rather, you are going to make them work hand-in-hand.

When you do use the monomyth or Hero's Journey context in your readings, take note of the square that has the most emphasis placed upon it (for example, if you have used the name method of choosing squares, the square with the most marks on it). This will indicate the starting point for the reading. If squares share an equal number of marks or emphasis, then the person for whom you are reading has energy and focus spread across those various themes and more focus is indicated in order to bring about quicker results.

Square 1 - The Call to Adventure

When this square is involved in a reading, our hero's center of focus has been shifted from what was once his ordinary world to "somewhere else." This emergence or starting point can appear either through the hero's own choice or from the hero having outside forces acting upon them. This is the stage that sets everything else into action and, as such, is appropriately inhabited by attributes that modify, shape, and amend the ordinary world.

Square 2 - Refusal of the Call

This square expresses to us that, once the call to adventure is awarded, the hero often refuses to follow it — even though it might, in fact, be a "roar" not just a "call." This is also about being silent and still once new information and wisdom is received. For this reason, this square is inhabited by attributes that contemplate, muse, and often stay soundless even though others think they should speak out.

Square 3 - Supernatural Aid

Help, caring, and nurturing are the attributes of this place of power. Having started on their quest, our hero receives the assistance of a parent figure or mentor. This "helping hand" protects as well as stimulates our hero. As such, this square is inhabited by attributes that serve as the genesis of individuality, sympathy for others, and the security of abundance.

Square 4 – Crossing the Threshold

This is the square that firmly establishes your hero's presence in the adventure that is unfolding. The person for whom you are reading has just met a protector and defender at the entrance to their new place of mastery and has been allowed to move in and move on. This square, then, is inhabited by attributes that speak of leadership, command, and dominion.

Square 5 – Belly of the Whale

The number 5 represents change, transformation, and the transitory nature of things. When this square is indicated in a reading, a conversion of sorts is called for. This is also the time when our hero is busy relating to the outside world (as opposed to bargaining with their own inner thoughts and desires). This square is also about being devoured or seemingly consumed by the facade of separation of our hero from their environment. Attributes that populate this square treat us to themes of evolution, tests, and challenges. This is a place of discoveries being made.

Square 6 – Meeting with the Goddess

When this square is indicated in a reading, our hero has met their ultimate trial – that of satisfying and giving fulfillment to one's heart. Here we find not only unconditional and absolute love of another, but the "love of one's fate" (the *amor fati* phrase used by Nietzsche). This is the place or stage whereat our hero accepts what the journey has brought and delivered. It is here that one finally sees the ultimate purpose of things. The skill, of course, is not being so enraptured and charmed that our lust diverts us from our odyssey.

Square 7 – The Ultimate Boon

Fundamentally, our hero has set out on their quest to find that blessing, that treasure, that goal that helps them to transcend or rise above the place from which they started. This is the place of power from which the charge is not only led but from which the treasure is realized. This battle brings with it the eventual understanding that the riches originally looked for may be more mystical than physical. While there are always reasons that can be found to go into battle, this square also speaks of having a worthy purpose in the first place. From this place, our hero's spirit and courage are tested one last time so that they can move past the act of conquering to a period of rest.

Square 8 – Master of the Two Worlds

This place of power along our hero's path represents self-determination and the ability to restrain what one sees through their eyes with what one dreams with the mind and spirit. There is a liberation and release in Square "8" that comes from the skillfulness of being able to walk and freely pass between the material and spiritual worlds. This square contains attributes that speak to us of removing barriers, prowess, and mastery over one's outlook on life, and the inspiration that permits the forcefulness of stillness in the face of the vigor of everyday life.

Square 9 – Freedom to Live

And so, we come to the final square of the adventure. Perhaps it is better to say this is the place that represents the deliverance from fear and regret. This is, then, a stage of bold and valiant determination to live in the present without regret from the past and concern of the future. Here we find our hero with self-rule and privilege while also knowing they are an expression of the world around them (the very thing they have been avoiding or breaking free from). This is our hero in their state as "more than a man." Here is someone who has learned how to live by dying again each day and being reborn anew. This square, appropriately, has the attributes of dreams actually lived – not just imagined, of the ability to be alone, but not lonely – of a revelation born from an acknowledgment of "what is."

PART TWELVE
MEDICINE WHEELS, THE MINOR ARCANA, AND STRUCTURES OF SELF

The future is no more uncertain than the present.

- Walt Whitman

Medicine Wheels

The hallowed concepts and connections that are commonly referred to as "medicine wheels" or "sacred hoops" bring extra wisdom and scope to your readings. These revered structures provide further elemental associations for each of the four directions. Indeed, there are many hidden and sublime structures of *The Vitruvian Square* - the delicate and precise formations within each square, itself. If you will consider the following preliminary diagram – a very simple Wheel of Be-Ing (Figure 40) – you will see that there can be perfect balance and symmetry in a person's life by focusing upon and using just the four coordinates of North, East, South, and West.

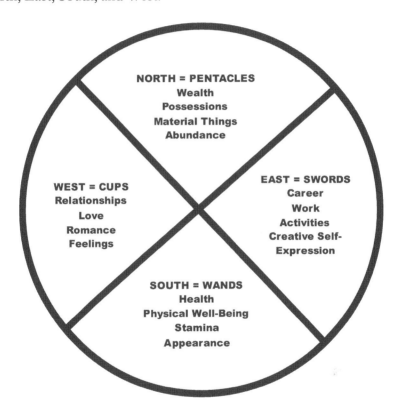

Figure 40 - The Wheel of Be-Ing

The origins of sacred or spiritual "wheels" – medicine wheels (sacred hoops), nature wheels, and life wheels – have been lost in antiquity and are attributed to various cultures and diverse time periods.

The simplest form of a wheel – a circle like the one in Figure 40 – is a symbol of unity; a state of no beginning and no ending, and of perfection. Each of the attributes in Figure 40 was carefully chosen from the numerous wisdoms of the ages.

If you intently consider each quarter of the wheel, those quarter's oppositions, and their neighbors, you will also discover how the four Minor Arcana suits of the Tarot literally play with and off of each other to form a cohesive whole; attributes that also appear in Figure 39.

The Minor Arcana

The Suits

There are four suits that comprise the Minor Arcana: Wands, Cups, Swords, and Pentacles. If you are using a regular deck of playing cards or my own *Deck of Shadows* these appear as the commonly known clubs, hearts, spades, and diamonds. Each of these symbols represents a different, specific, and exclusive action, place, thing, or person. If nothing else, it will assist you in your readings to consider the following attributes for these four identifiers within *The Vitruvian Square*.

Swords / Spades

The suit of Swords is associated with the element of Air, the direction of East, and the color Yellow. It is the suit of thinking and rationality. On the wheel it is directly opposite the suit of Cups.

A sword is a weapon of cutting and thrusting. It is a symbol of power, influence, and force. Sometimes, its mere appearance or display is enough to change things and people. A sword changes futures. As such, this suit can also be a sign or indication of loss, delay, and disappointment.

The various correspondences/keywords for Swords in a reading would be:

Spirit

Creativity

Accept

Autonomy

Yellow

Air

"I Take"

"I Will"

"I Think"

The East

Work/Ambition

The Past (Lessons)

"What Could Have Been"

"What Was"

Birth/Rebirth

Mental

Springtime

Wands / Clubs

The suit of Wands is associated with the element of Fire, the direction of South, and the color Red. It is the suit of intuition and energy. On the wheel it is directly opposite the suit of Pentacles.

A wand is something ceremonial (even if nothing more than a twig or rod). More than a mere bauble, it is an emblem of those who control, protect, and create – sometimes to the extent of producing phenomena not ordinarily in accordance with what is currently thought to be the laws of nature. A wand can be otherworldly to others.

The various correspondences/keywords for Wands in a reading would be:

Body

Faith

Build

Spirituality

Red

Fire

"I Have"

"I Need"

"I Intuit"

The South

Health/Physical

The Soul

Harmony

"What Has Always Been"

Growth

Spiritual

Summertime

Cups / Hearts

The suit of Cups is associated with the Alchemical element of Water, the direction of West, and the color Blue. It is the suit of feelings, affection, relations, and emotions. On the wheel it is directly opposite the suit of Swords.

A cup is something that holds another thing. It can be filled. It can be overfilled. It can be emptied only to be filled again. The container does not change, but its contents can be anything. When you look into a cup, you see what was placed there or emptied in the past.

The various correspondences/keywords for Cups in a reading would be:

Heart

Dreams

Impart

Union

Blue

Water

"I Give"

"I Can"

"I Feel"

The West

Love/Romance

Harvesting

Visions

"What If . . ."

Feeling

Fall

Pentacles / Diamonds

The suit of Pentacles is associated with the element of Earth, the direction of North, and the color Green. It is the suit of sensations, acquisitions, and material things. On the wheel it is directly opposite the suit of Wands.

A pentacle is a star with 5 points. Used in Tarot, it is also a coin; a common medium of exchange, an indicator of wealth, and a system of acceptance between people. "Currency" also has the feeling of "nowness."

The various correspondences/keywords for Pentacles in a reading would be:

Mind

Wisdom

Preserve

Stability

Green

Earth

"I Hold"

"I Want"

"I Sense"

The North

Possessions/Finances

The Present

Realities

"What Is"

Achievement

Physical

Wintertime

Bringing this all together, what follows is a table of

correspondences for the four quarters. This summary will be useful in your further exploration and show you just how interrelated all the

various aspects are with each other.

TABLE OF CORRESPONDENCES

	EAST	SOUTH	WEST	NORTH
Playing Card	Spades	Clubs	Hearts	Diamonds
Ego Function	Thinking	Intuition	Feeling	Sensation
Stage of Life	Youth	Young Adult	Maturity	Old Age
Seasonal Cycle	Spring (March / April / May)	Summer (June / July / August)	Fall (September / October / November)	Winter (December / January / February)
Daily Cycle	Morning	Noon	Evening	Night
Life Cycle	Birth/Rebirth	Growth	Harvesting	Achievement
Significance	Loss	Power	Love	Life
Time (1)	Past (Lessons / "What Could Have Been")	Soul (Harmony / "What Has Always Been")	Future (Visions / "What if")	Present (Realities / "What is")
Time (2)	When	Always	Then	Now
Location	There	Everywhere	If	Here
Health Aspect	Mental	Spiritual	Emotional	Physical
Divine Aspect	Spirit	Body	Heart	Mind
Mental Aspect	Creativity	Faith	Dreams	Wisdom
Intent	Accept	Build	Impart	Preserve
The Search	Autonomy	Spirituality	Unity	Stability
Color	Yellow (Skill)	Red (Blood)	Blue (Passion)	Green (Currency)
Element	Air	Fire	Water	Earth
Purpose	"To Take"	"To Have"	"To Give"	"To Hold"
Demand	Will	Need	Can	Want

	EAST	SOUTH	WEST	NORTH
Minor Arcana	Swords	Wands	Cups	Pentacles
Life Theme	Work / Ambition / Career	Health / Physical / Well-Being	Love / Sex / Relationships	Possessions / Finances / Wealth
Thinking Style	Logical / Factual	Conceptual / Visual	Emotional / Musical	Sequential / Detailed
State of Being	Waking	Aware	Celebrating	Thoughtful
Energy Source	Activities	Stamina	Romance	Material Things
Outcome	Creative Self-Expression	Appearance	Desire	Abundance

The Structures of Self

As you have seen, there are cardinal, directional associations for each of the orientations within a medicine wheel (East = Swords = Air, South = Wands = Fire, West = Cups = Water, North = Pentacles = Earth). Expanding on this still further, you can also incorporate Jungian archetypes; recurrent models of behavior, thinking, and feeling that indicate how a person will react and respond in the world. Dr. Carl Jung, building on the concepts of Plato and Greek philosophy, believed that there were deeper mythological levels or patterns within both the individual and our collective unconsciousness. In addition to suggesting that events in a person's life are standard (much the same as we explored earlier in the Hero's Journey and mythic reading technique), Dr. Jung advised that the collective experience of people resulted in ingrained and

deep-rooted patterns of thought and symbols. Dr. Jung suggested the

following archetypal models:

The Father/Mother = Security = Ruling/Nurturing

The Hero = Freedom = Rescuing/Defending

The Magician = Uncertainty = Mysterious/Deceiving

The Maiden = Belonging = Desire/Enjoyment

Using updated terminology from Dr. Robert Moore and Douglas

Gillette in their elaboration on Dr. Jung's work, I suggest that we have

the following associations to work with for each Place of Power that rests

inside *The Vitruvian Square*:

East = Warrior (Hero)

South = Magician

West = Lover (Maiden)

North = King/Queen (Father/Mother)

An example of what has just been described using Square 1 as an

example looks like this (Figure 41):

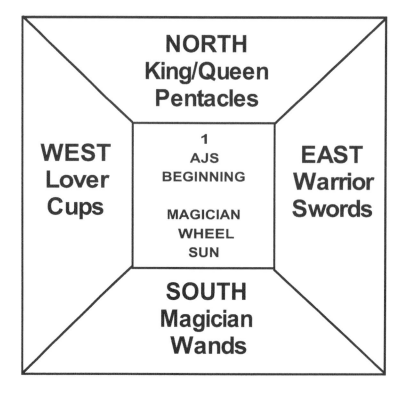

**Figure 41 - A Sample Medicine Wheel Structure within The
Vitruvian Square using Square 1**

Identical layouts exist for each of the remaining eight Places of

Power (Squares 2 through 9). You will be using these nine different

wheels to further expand your readings and add more detail. In other

words, you will focus on a particular square of your choosing and then

intuitively take notice of the direction within that square that seems to be

calling to you. Using Figure 41, as an example, you might get a sense that

the east end of the square is drawing your attention. In a reading you will not only talk about the attributes of the number 1 and the various Tarot card connections with that location, you will also discuss the distinctions represented by The Warrior, Swords, and The East. Because we are using Square 1 for this example, you will now talk about "beginnings" and a magician's intent in the context of using one's intellect and mind (the additional overlay of Air/Swords). You will also discuss The Magician's concentration and training; his aid and care (The Warrior aspect).

To further assist you in easily operating within *The Vitruvian Square* with the concepts of this chapter, the following explanations are given. If some of these notions and interpretations are beginning to sound similar to topics already covered, that should be no surprise. *The Vitruvian Square*, you will recall, is essentially a marriage of numerous theories that were previously thought to be separate (but which are not).

North

North is the place of repose and dominion. It is the place of the coldest season – Winter; that time of year when we go "home" to experience what we already have and to start a rebirth for what is to come. It is a time for celebration and observing. It is during this time of year that we receive emotional comfort and a soothing lull.

This is the realm of the King and Queen, the monarch, and the ruler. Recognition, resolution, and command are important. Truth and standards are the foundation for all actions. Control and nurturing are critical in this type of person's decision-making process. Our sovereign wants to command and parent. The King and Queen, unbroken, ask us, "How may I lead you?"

East

East is the place of the sunrise and, hence, the start of a new day. It is from here that we "see the light"; when we gain understanding or a new belief. From here we gain sudden insights and thus change for the better (at least so we think). The mind gains its energy from the lifting of darkness the East represents.

This place is the morning field of battle for The Warrior, the fighter, and the champion. This is the place from which an offense is launched and a defense intensified. This is an individual who is both possessive and protective of the people and the property around them. Our combatant wants to stand up for a purpose and a belief so that his victory is deserved. This hero wants to prove their worth. The Warrior asks us, "How may I defend you?"

South

South is the place of fire and burning. This is a time of growth and expansion; of progress and advancement. There are no shadows when the Sun is at its highest point. Thus, this is a time for mastery and understanding and proficiency. Dignity, honor, and self-esteem also find their homes in the South. This is also the time when healing occurs and things are made "right" and balance is restored.

The South is the theatre of The Magician, the director, and the architect. Creativity, originality and imagination take precedence here. This is an individual who prizes their individuality and ability to show their talent and skill. They thrive on uncovering and mastering the secrets of the universe. Our enchanter wants to fascinate and enthrall. The Magician delightfully asks us, "How may I charm you?"

West

West is the time of Fall and the setting Sun. It is time for reaping what has previously been sown and realizing the benefits of prior endeavors. This is the time when we collect what we know and put it to concerted use and effect. However, it is also a place of melancholy and dissatisfaction with the way things and people are. It is in the West that we realize we have reached the prime of our life and now have old age before us. From this place, we give thanks for what has been achieved and the abundance we have been shown.

This is the playground of The Lover, the partner, and the companion. Affection, feelings, and tenderness compel this type of individual forward. This is a person who thrives on empathy and intimacy. This is an individual who gives in to self-indulgence and relishes bringing others fleshly enjoyment. Our darling wants bliss and to rejoice. The Lover impishly asks us, "How may I pleasure you?"

As I mentioned before, once you become very familiar with these concepts, you will be internally drawn to one portion of a particular square over another during a reading. All you need do is direct your attention to the square you want to use and then imagine one area of that square and bring your attention to that location. With that intent and purpose in mind, you are then able to further refine a reading for someone.

The Deck of Shadows

Earlier, I referenced *The Deck of Shadows*. I trust you will permit me the short indulgence of adding a final portion to this chapter that expands on using that particular deck with *The Vitruvian Square*. *The Deck of Shadows* is particularly well-suited for use with the medicine wheel application to *The Vitruvian Square*. Each of *The Deck of Shadows* cards can be viewed, meditated upon, and used as you would with the Minor Arcana from the Tarot; an extension or radiating arm from its Major Arcana or numerological base.

Briefly, take each set of the four similarly numbered cards (e.g., the four Aces, four Twos, four Threes, etc.) and lay them out in their respective orientations within each numbered square. In other words, the Ace of Diamonds represents the North, the Ace of Spades represents the East, the Ace of Clubs represents the South, and the Ace of Hearts represents the West. You can then use the meanings for each of the oracle cards to add further significance to the square being used for the reading.

When using the Jacks, Queens, and Kings, their equivalent numbers are:

JACKS = 2 (11 or 1 + 1)

QUEENS = 3 (12 or 1 + 2)

KINGS = 4 (13 or 1 + 3)

To further assist you, here is an example of *The Deck of Shadows* being used with location 1 in *The Vitruvian Square* (Figure 42):

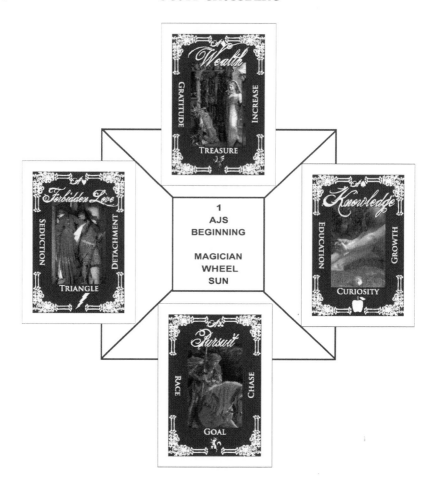

**Figure 42 - The Deck of Shadow "Aces" in
The Vitruvian Square**

You can, of course, use any set of cards (other oracle decks or a

standard deck of playing cards) provided they have numbers on them

that can be applied to the various places of power within *The Vitruvian*

Square. I prefer using *The Deck of Shadows* because, in addition to the

number and suit equivalents on the cards, I have the power to include the various meanings of the individual cards.

The Rubber Band Spread

As you start using the medicine wheel concept and the various cardinal points, you might want to consider using an instructive and deeply powerful layout based on something called "The Rubber Band Model." I first learned of this rubber band concept in the book entitled "The Decision Book" by Mikael Krogerus and Roman Tschappeler. Robert A. Burgelman of the Stanford Graduate School of Business has opined on a like-minded, more complex, but similarly named model (he called his model "The Rubber Band Phenomenon"). Similarly, you might find Michael Porter's six key forces for corporate strategy an interesting review and perhaps basis of further layout ideas.

Simply, imagine that you are being pulled in four directions by rubber bands and you must hold equal pressure in all directions to maintain harmony (to stay centered between the four forces). With this type of structure, you must come to terms with the fact that you are being drawn to somewhere else and being held in place all at the same time.

The first direction is to the East (Air/Emperor). This is the direction you are pulled because of the way you talk to yourself internally (how you are internally programming yourself).

The second direction is to the South (Fire/Judgement). This is the direction you are pulled by what it will take for you to win (your plan of action).

The third direction is to the West (Water/Lovers). This is the direction you are pulled by your activities (what you actually do in furtherance of your plan of action).

The fourth direction is to the North (Earth/High Priestess). This is the direction you are pulled by the environment in which you find yourself (your chosen reality).

When a reading involves a decision that must be made, realize that the person being read must constantly consider these four directions and elements. You can use The Rubber Band Layout to help determine how best for the person being read to stay in balance. Here's how to put this into play:

STEP 1: From a face-up Tarot deck or *The Deck of Shadows*, purposefully choose a card that represents the situation in which the person being read finds himself or herself. Place it face-up in front of you in the place that would occupy Square 5 of *The Vitruvian Square* matrix (Change/Hierophant).

STEP 2: Mix and cut the cards until you are content.

STEP 3: Ask the question: "What is keeping this person adaptable?" Deal one card face-up to the left of your original chosen card. This will be Square 4 of *The Vitruvian Square* (East/Air/Emperor). This card represents the enticement of listening to your own inner monologue.

STEP 4: Ask the question: "What is keeping this person inflexible?" Deal one card face-up below your original chosen card. This will be Square 8 of *The Vitruvian Square* (South/Fire/Judgement). This card represents the pull of a battle plan.

STEP 5: Ask the question: "What is forcing this person away from where they are?" Deal one card face-up to the right of your original chosen card. This will be Square 6 of *The Vitruvian Square* (West/Water/Lovers). This card represents the attraction of moving in a new direction, take risks, and change.

STEP 6: Ask the question: "What is holding this person in place?" Deal one card face-up above your original chosen card. This will be Square 2 of *The Vitruvian Square* (North/Earth/High Priestess). This card represents the temptation to keep the status quo and stay where you are.

STEP 7: Notice the four cards that are the powers that are enticing, pulling, attracting, and tempting the card in the middle. Ask yourself how you feel about each one and give that reading. For example, you might consider what happens for your sitter when these four cards each pull in their respective direction? What is the "snapping point" – the point at which a particular card's tension breaks – for each card? What can your sitter do to decrease the tension of any particular card?

STEP 8: After discussion with the person being read, determine which one of the four outer cards will rock your sitter's world if they go in that direction. Which of the cards feels like it is more intense, enabling, and potent than the other? Which card represents the strongest force? You can do a separate reading on that card, as well.

PART THIRTEEN
ALCHEMY AND VESSELS OF THE SOUL

The alchemists spent years in their laboratories,

observing the fire that purified the metals.

They spent so much time close to the fire that

gradually they gave up the vanities of the world.

They discovered that the purification of the metals

had led to a purification of themselves.

- Paulo Coehlo, *The Alchemist*

Now we move into a fascinating and truly fun aspect of *The Vitruvian Square* and a subject that I believe truly underscores the unified nature of this "reading" approach. Using the following techniques, there is no doubt that you will transform your readings into something magical. One warning: This will be the most arcane and grand discussion, yet. Still . . .

. . . imagine your reading skills at the next level. What if, without fail, you are able to give a reading that highlights someone's true essence - their unique combination of dynamic and resistant aspects? Just suppose you are able to provide insights that include how a person is overcome by and conquers the daily happenings of life. What this means to you is the ability to provide a reading that is unlike anything others are currently giving. You will be able to personalize the use of the following applications like no other aspect previously discussed.

Of utmost importance to me in applying the principles of Alchemy to *The Vitruvian Square* are the sacred unions that take place when the various Places of Power are mixed with one another in an attempt to transmute the Sitter and thus achieve ultimate enlightenment - something I will discuss under the section entitled, The Unity of Opposites, below. While the Rosicrucians proffered a "sevenfold soul of man," I offer here nine Vehicles of the Soul; each one corresponding to a different location within *The Vitruvian Square* and fully coordinated with each of the principles already addressed. You will be amazed to see how congruent this all becomes with the prior, offered concepts.

I must explain, first, that I am not concerned here with the physical act of turning a clump of cool lead into the warmth and richness of gold. This is about personal, philosophical, spiritual, and psychological Alchemy and its application to readings. It is as much about the way individuals relate to each other as it is about how a person relates to himself or herself. This aspect of *The Vitruvian Square* allows you to outline for another person how they dream internally and how that individual's personal journey to perfection can be aided.

In Part Twelve of the book ("MEDICINE WHEELS, ORACLES, AND STRUCTURES OF THE SELF"), I discussed duality and the use of Medicine Wheels with *The Vitruvian Square*; an indispensable part of any reading. Think of what is to follow as an expansion of that concept. You already know the technique of selecting the Squares of Power to use and how to apply the standard associations with each of the directions (East - Swords, South - Wands, West - Cups, North - Pentacles). You will now be taking your understanding far beyond what other readers think possible; namely, you will be giving a transformational reading that carefully unpeels your Sitter layer by layer.

Before I show you *The Vitruvian Square* in all its alchemical glory, let us discuss a few basic concepts.

Prima Materia

(The First Matter)

The nine squares that make up *The Vitruvian Square*, itself, when viewed as a whole, are a representation of the Prima Materia or First Matter. Think of the nine squares as building blocks that can be assembled to create reality. Alchemists will tell you that all matter is ordered, formed, or created out of this original elemental chaos. When the various components of the Prima Materia are discovered or reunited, those portions make up what someone sees, experiences, feels, and imagines during their everyday life. In doing your readings with *The Vitruvian Square*, you will be separating out the Prima Materia (the nine squares) into active and passive elements of a person's life. Obviously, there is no fixed combination of dynamic and peaceful parts that is identical and applicable to everyone; each person has his or her own personal balance to address, react to, and create from the nine components presented by *The Vitruvian Square*.

I also hasten to add that, in the realms of philosophical esotericism and esoteric writing, it was common for an author to relay their thoughts "between the lines." This is certainly true of the alchemical mysteries. Accordingly, I invite you to consider that, when we explore passive and active elements, we are not just talking about a binary split between male and female designations. Rather, the direct (active) and cyclic (passive) energies work together and are found in each of us. As you read through the following explanations consider that the discussion is more about how a person expresses their personal energy and what can be done to keep such energy in balance.

The Prima Materia, then, is the fundamental frame within which you will construct a reading and, as it is used with *The Vitruvian Square*, is made up of The Four Elements and The Four Essentials. These eight essences are held together and made knowable through Spirit (or the remaining place of power at Square 5).

The Four Elements: These are the fundamental and absolute ingredients or constituents of all matter and are born from The Four Essentials. They are (1) Earth (Square 2), (2) Air (Square 6), (3) Fire (Square 8), and (4) Water (Square 4). To each is assigned a conforming and overriding characteristic or power. Thus, Earth is dominantly cold, Air is prevailingly dry, Fire is loomingly hot, and Water is unquestionably wet. You will notice that these four elements are befittingly located in the places of power that make up the Diamond of Harmony.

You will immediately notice that these Four Elements are incapable of directly turning into each other. Fire cannot turn into Water, Earth, or Air on its own. Rather, any transformation requires a careful compounding and mixing of elements. For example, Fire and Water make steam, or Earth and Fire make magma. I encourage you to go back and look at my discussion of medicine wheels and you will see the inception of this "mixing" concept.

The Four Elements are comprised of passive and active characteristics; features you will use in a reading to explain what is happening in someone's life and why those things are occurring. Air and Fire are active, light, and generally move in an upward direction (Heaven-bound). Water and Earth are passive, heavy and move in a downward direction (Earth-bound).

The Four Essentials: Where the Four Elements are the components of matter, the Four Essentials are forces that make up and are the birthplace for the balance of existence. These are comprised of (1) Primal Mud (Square 1), (2) Salt (Square 3), (3) Sulphur (Square 9), and (4) Quicksilver (Square 7). Original texts only recognize Three Essentials (or Three Supernals) - omitting the Primal Mud. However, the principles embodied within *The Vitruvian Square* recognize that the original Three

Essentials could not exist without a starting place - the Primal Mud (or the gross material from which life is born). Each of The Four Essentials is also assigned a matching correspondence: Primal Mud - Beginning, Sulphur - Ending, Salt – Creating, and Quicksilver - Destroying. You will see that The Four Essentials are contained within the places of power that make up the Diamond of Chaos.

The Four Essentials, too, are comprised of passive and active characteristics. Primal Mud (made up of Water and Earth) and Quicksilver (made up of Fire and Water) are passive. Salt (made up of Earth and Air) and Sulphur (made up of Fire and Air) are active.

As opposed to The Four Elements, The Four Essentials are not fixed. Indeed, The Four Essentials are capable of existing in more than one form or manifest as more than one identifiable power. The Four Essentials are capable of mixing with other elements and creating dynamics greater than the sum of their parts.

Spirit (Luna): You will also see that Square 5 contains the symbol of Silver or the Spirit; that which animates and inspires and shifts the other locations, elements, and attributes. Think of this place of power as the meeting point or place of convergence for the other squares and that which seeks to move everything upward towards the Ultima Materia.

Ultima Materia

(The Magical Child)

Alchemists believe that the practice of combining the correct and measured ingredients from the Prima Materia results in the birth of The Magical Child (*filius sapientiae* or *filius philosophorum*); also known as the reborn self. Some have equated this resulting power with The Philosopher's Stone (*lapis philosophorum*); that powerful object or concept that has the ability to transform anything that is connected with it.

For our purposes in giving readings, the use of the Ultima Materia is twofold. First, it is the Holy Grail of existence, wisdom, and understanding that our Sitter seeks to attain. Second, it is the resulting transformation - the goal - of our Sitter as he or she travels through life and moves from the material to the spiritual.

The Alchemical Vitruvian Square

So, finally with this background in place, let us see what *The Alchemical Vitruvian Square* looks like (Figure 43):

VEHICLES OF THE SOUL

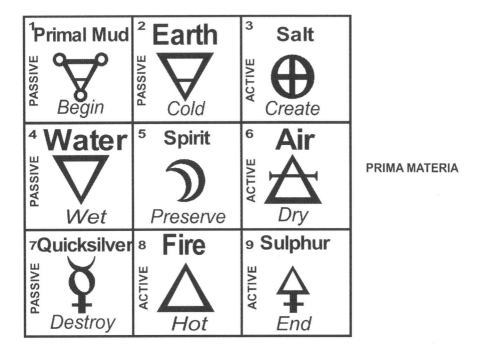

Figure 43 - The Alchemical Vitruvian Square

Selecting the various squares to interpret using my alchemical model is no different than I discussed originally for use with other divination options. Whether you use the letters of a person's name, a birth date, intuition, the selections of cards, or any other of numerous and varied choices, you ultimately are left with certain squares highlighted and others unselected.

Let's revisit the use of the name, "RICHARD DRACO."

Applying the letters of that name to *The Vitruvian Square* (this time with an alchemical theme) we get (Figure 44):

VEHICLES OF THE SOUL

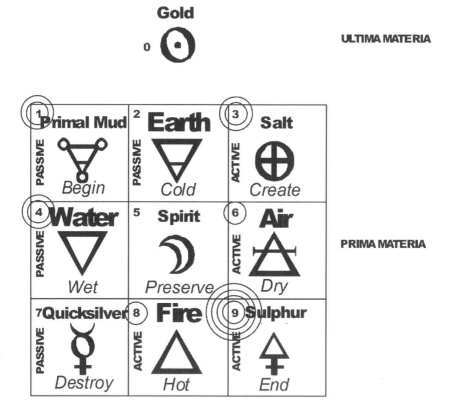

Figure 44 - The Name "Richard Draco" Applied to
The Alchemical Vitruvian Square

I will explain in a moment how I would interpret this. But first, let's explore a few more concepts that I use to add an alchemical flair to my readings.

Coincidental Oppositorum

(The Unity of Opposites / The Coincidence of Opposites)

Whether you adhere to the old adage that the world is made up of opposites or you stand by Newton's law of motion that says, "To every action there is always an equal and opposite reaction," mankind has long been enamored by dualistic cosmology. Alchemy is certainly no different.

I am confident you have noticed by now that *The Vitruvian Square* is intentionally composed of connections of opposites. Fire (hot) is opposite to Earth (cold). Air (dry) is opposite to Water (wet). These elements, by the way, are consistent with the psychological constructs of thinking (Air), feeling (Water), intuition (Fire), and sensation (Earth).

Just as the Four Elements are in opposition to each other, so are the Four Essentials. Primal Mud (Beginning) is opposite to Sulphur (Ending). Salt (Creating) is opposite to Quicksilver (Destroying).

You will also see that each of the elements and essentials is connected to the other through Square 5 - The Spirit. The Place of

Power, for the Spirit, is naturally the center of *The Vitruvian Square* and seeks to enlighten by showing the oneness of everything. It is through the preserving nature of Square 5 that the other squares are allowed to mix and unify without fear of losing their own individuality in the process. It is through this Spirit that we begin to see that everything is connected and there is a revelation of identicalness in those things we previously thought separate and apart.

Now, take a look back at Figure 44, above, and imagine the various elements and essences that are assigned to each location. Imagine what happens when the various items begin to mix, blend, dance, and combine with each other. We all know what happens when too much water is poured on a fire; the fire is extinguished and you are left with smoke and a soggy mess. When that same fire is impacted by too much wind, the air currents either extinguish the flames or, more probably, fan them into a raging storm of their own. By the same token when earth is added to a fire, the fire smolders quietly beneath the soil with the ever-present risk that the flames will reignite at a later, unexpected time. These same analogies hold true when The Four Elements attempt to cross-over onto and into each other.

Continuing with our example, when too much emotion or feeling (Water) is added to a person's intuition (Fire), that person's instinctive, unemotional knowing can vaporize and resemble a watery mess of confusion. Remember: "I just have a feeling" is different than the impressions of intuition so don't confuse emotions and intuition with each other. (As a side note, if you were nonetheless to consider feelings and intuition as the same – either both Water elements or both Fire elements – you would then have either a flood of emotion or the outburst of a fire storm.) When that same intuition (Fire) is touched by too much thinking (Air), suddenly intuition (the knowing without reason or feeling) is either suppressed or, alternatively, there is a backlash of unpredictable hunches that result.

Likewise, in this example, when sensations (Earth) are added to a person's intuition (Fire), that intuition, yet again, is suppressed beneath the weight of the external world.

As you can now see, the various combinations result in very predictable and understandable outcomes. These foreseeable results also serve as the bases for very detailed readings. While I encourage you to meditate upon the various elemental and essential combinations and what you already know from your observations of the world around you, the following may get you started:

EARTH (Square 2)

With this element you have manifestation and material creation, possessions, and wealth represented. This is what keeps "your feet on the ground" and causes you to embrace the need for security. This element wants to hold you and be held. Earth is firm and solid and gives us a connection – even when it shakes, rattles, and rolls. It is a place to rest. Cold on its own, it becomes many other things when mixed with other elements. At its core, Earth is the "Abode of Mortals." It is a feminine/passive aspect of a person.

Earth is associated with the Tarot Major Arcana of The High Priestess (II), Justice (XI), and Judgement (XX).

Mixed with:

Air – Earth dries out and can be blown and tossed about. However, Air is needed for things to flourish and grow from Earth.

Fire – Earth and Fire are opposite elements of each other. Earth can become scorched and unsalvageable by Fire. Yet, Earth cannot only contain Fire, it can smother the Fire, taking away its source of food (Air), and ultimately extinguishing it. If not quenched entirely by the Earth's covering, Fire will smolder.

Water – Earth and Water, in proper balance, are intimate playmates for Water makes Earth fertile and productive. However, Water, in excess, can flood Earth causing mud, muck, and mire. Earth, in excess, soaks up Water until it is gone.

AIR (Square 6)

Here you have Spirit brought to Earth and an ascension back again. Air represents the mind, speech, and words consciously used. This element gives rise to the need for expression and sharing. In fact, the word "air" means more than the mere element. Think about how many times we use phrases like "there was an air of secrecy about her" or "I just want to air our differences" or, in a television or radio setting, "we're on the air." If you "air your differences," you are making something public. All of these examples ultimately refer to something that is being communicated. Indeed, many of you have heard the lyric, "The answer, my friend, is blowin' in the wind." This element is visionary and sometimes not easily grasped and it can bring the "winds of change." Air is required for breathing and sustains life once that life is born to the Earth. It can be refreshing if there is a slight breeze. Indeed, don't we "air out the house?" While some texts refer to Air as neutral, I submit that it is, in actuality, a masculine/active aspect of a person.

Air is associated with the Tarot Major Arcana of The Lovers (VI) and The Devil (XV).

Mixed with:

Earth – See above.

Fire – Air feeds and fans a Fire, making it stronger, hotter, and more vibrant. Too much Air and the flames are blown out or, alternatively, become a fire-storm which, in turn, creates its own winds from the excessive and oppressive heat.

Water – Air and Water are opposite elements of each other. Water can turn the Air moist and wet. Air can carry Water away. If Air is added to Water, the Water becomes excited; carbonated, effervescent, or fermented. If too much Water is added to Air, we are deprived of our ability to breathe.

FIRE (Square 8)

Fire provides activity, transformation, willpower, courage, and strength. This is the "spark" that ignites you, gets you up early in the morning, and keeps you up late at night. Fire is intense, and always moving, and arouses others – not just your Sitter – to action. It can burn if it gets too close; it is hot and destructive. Fire also gives off light which, of course, creates shadows – its own sort of darkness. Fire can be used to terminate or discharge something as in "you're fired" or "they fired their weapons." It also protects and is used to mark territory. It can be used to cook and prepare nourishment and sustenance for someone. It also can be a severe trial "by fire." It is a masculine aspect of a person.

Fire is associated with the Tarot Major Arcana of Strength (VIII), and The Star (XVII).

Mixed with:

Air – See above.

Earth – See above.

Water – While, on first blush, these would appear to be opposite elements, they are not. However, Fire can cause Water to reach a boiling state and turn into steam. The steam can either be harnessed for energy or burn by scalding. Water can drench Fire and douse its light.

WATER (Square 4)

This element is cleansing and purifying. It represents the "flow" of love, emotions, and the subconscious. Water is not only necessary for life, it is a cast-off or by-product of all living things in the form of, among other things, waste, tears, and sweat. In life, water always seeks its own balance. It has the ability to creep into tiny crevices and, given enough time, wear down even the largest stone. Water is reflective and is a mirror of the things that touch, look into, and come near it. As such, it can be deceptively shallow or deep and change its colors. It cools and refreshes us when we are too hot or too tired. We can drown in it, not because we have fallen into it or experience it, but because we fail to get back out. As has been said, you can't stand in the same river twice, because it is always flowing and changing. It is a feminine aspect of a person.

Water is associated with the Tarot Major Arcana of The Emperor (IV), and Death (XIII).

Mixed with:

Air – See above.

Fire – See above.

Earth – See above.

SPIRIT (Square 5)

This is not one of The Four Elements nor one of The Four Essentials. Rather, it is the presence, belief, and movement towards perfection. It seeks material manifestation through its interaction with each and every one of the other Places of Power.

Spirit is associated with the Tarot Major Arcana of The Hierophant (V) and Temperance (XIV).

PRIMAL MUD (Square 1)

This Essential is brought about by the combination of the only two tangible elements: Earth and Water. Because Earth is cool and Water is wet, this clay of life is fluid and unstable.

Primal Mud is associated with the Tarot Major Arcana of The Magician (I), The Wheel of Fortune (X), and The Sun (XIX).

SALT (Square 3)

This Essential is the combination of Earth and Air. It is what ancient Alchemists thought to be the frail beginning of things and something that must be ultimately destroyed or dissolved to release a thing's true essence.

Salt is associated with the Tarot Major Arcana of The Empress (III), The Hanged Man (XII), and The World (XXI).

SULPHUR (Square 9)

This Essential is the intense and fiery combination of Fire and Air. This is the essence of active energy and is what results or is left over and extracted from everything else.

Sulphur is associated with the Tarot Major Arcana of The Hermit (IX) and The Moon (XVIII).

QUICKSILVER (Square 7)

This Essential is the watery and feminine combination of Fire and Water. It is the obscure but powerful side of life.

Quicksilver is associated with the Tarot Major Arcana of The Chariot (VII) and The Tower (XVI).

GOLD (0)

Alchemists believe that the most eminent and pure substance is Gold. Attaining Gold was thought to be the ultimate goal of alchemical practice. As I have said before, the goal of mankind is to move from the material to the spiritual. Think of "Gold" as the spiritual aspect of that purpose. Thus, Gold is not only what we strive for (either consciously or unconsciously) but that which operates quietly and oftentimes concealed and which continues to advance all of the other Places of Power forward.

Gold is associated with the Tarot Major Arcanum of The Fool (O).

From the brief examples and explanations previously discussed, you should be able to see the analogies that are readily available to you in giving readings. Keep in mind that these Elements and Essentials and Spirit all dance with each other continually. So, keep your readings just as fluid and variable. While *The Vitruvian Square* is fixed, the application,

importance, and interaction of Elements and Essentials within the image

are not. Indeed, this Universe made of Elements and Essentials is in

constant change - a crucial distinction for you to use in providing

empowering readings.

I do not present readings to anyone and claim that anything is

"fixed." Rather, I offer the possibility that what I am seeing is an

indication of the way things were, are, and will be. I also quickly explain

that everything we are discussing can be changed (and I am ready to help

them see the methods for those changes to take place).

Ultimately, your aim in reading using *The Vitruvian Square* will be

to restore or find balance for people so that they are free to move to the

next level of accomplishment, emotion, and development. By simply

determining which Places of Power will be highlighted for use during a

reading, you have a very visual tool for seeing what is out of balance for

your Sitter.

Putting It All Together

Now, let us explore *The Vitruvian Square* with its alchemical

overlay for the name, "RICHARD DRACO." As a reminder, here is

what we have after each of the letters of the name was plotted:

VEHICLES OF THE SOUL

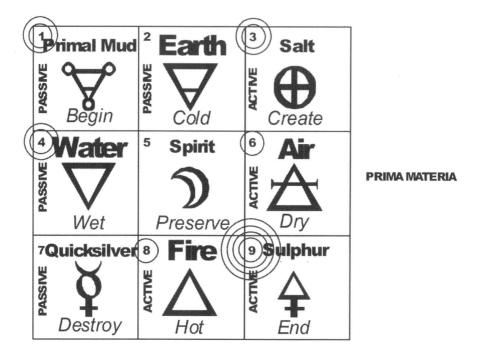

On first blush here is what I observe and what can be said from

an alchemical viewpoint:

It is obvious that the major, essential abstract in your life

is the need to stay active – but in a new way each and every time.

You are constantly leaving one thing behind in order to mix with

and create something else. You thrive on bringing things to a conclusion, to an end. In doing so, you essentially find yourself all over again and are reborn.

You also operate firmly in the Past and find that your memories spur you to action in the Present and Future. You would be well-served, however, to concentrate more on the Here and Now rather than allowing the Past to continue to spill over you.

I note that you don't seem to operate fully in any of the planes of existence. In other words, you are constantly being somewhat flighty. This is confirmed by your lack of any presence in the Earth place of power; another indication that you need to be grounded in the Present in order to become fully powerful.

You are equally represented in the areas of Air, Fire, and Water with a little more emphasis on your emotions (Water) than the others. However, because of all the other "active" items, I think you will agree that every time you allow your emotions to dictate your next course of conduct or you fall prey to your feelings, you begin to feel sluggish and inactive.

Your Axis of Power is missing the concept of Spirit and the drive to maintain and conserve yourself. Perhaps you would be best served by bringing your conscious intent to focus upon keeping what you have built intact and using that former creation to bolster what you will be doing in the Future. As I said earlier, you tend to jump from one thing to another – leaving "What Was" behind (ironic since you are so Past-oriented) in favor of "What Will Be." Essentially, you are someone who gets a thrill and a rush from starting out on projects. Learn to delight in the final result as much as in the act of doing.

Finally, it appears that in order to place your intention and attention more into the Future, you need to develop a Quicksilver or mercurial aspect to your personality. You might think you are already doing this because of your constant comings and goings and new creations. However, your current life strategy is supported by your intent to have control at all times – hence the strong presence of The Primal Mud and Salt in you. If you will be but a little more unpredictable and learn to relish sudden changes as much as you are pleased with the concept of controlled variety, you will suddenly find the balance and freedom you know you want.

Once again, these are just some basic thoughts to show you how this unique aspect of *The Vitruvian Square* can be used. There are more nuances and subtleties to be applied and I urge you to continue to meditate upon each Place of Power and their various correspondences.

The Stages of Vitruvian Transformation

Finally, there are as many alchemical process outlines and techniques as there appear to be writers on the subject. I have seen as many as 109 unique steps listed and as few as 7 viable ones. For our purposes with *The Vitruvian Square*, I am going to concentrate on only nine series of changes or transformations as they coincide superbly with the attributes we have already studied for the nine Places of Power. In other words, the nine alchemical processes outlined below are consistent and correspond with each of the numbers 1 through 9. This correlation (Figure 45) assists you in adding even more depth to your readings.

1 CALCINATION	2 DISSOLUTION	3 SEPARATION
4 CONJUNCTION	5 MORTI- FICATION	6 FERMENTA- TION
7 COMBUSTION	8 DISTILLATION	9 COAGULATION

Figure 45 - The Stages of
The Alchemical Vitruvian Square

As we explore these series of alchemical steps, pay particular attention to the cycles of birth and death, delivery and rest, and beginnings and endings that serve as continual themes.

Square 1 – Calcination

This is the process of beginning the alchemical transformation. It involves undergoing or causing a reaction by applying heat (in this case, the intensity of feeling and attention). The observation and examination of one's own mental, emotional, and physical actions take place when this fire of the imagination and original ideas is sparked. Once the heat of this process is applied, normal existence ceases.

If Square 1 is indicated during a reading, you would comment on the raging fire that exists within the person for whom you are reading. This is the time when a person's creative energies are brought to the surface in one of two forms – actual and potential. In other words, the person receiving the reading is at a turning point (a new beginning) whereby something is actually started or, alternatively, something is possible but further energy must be directed to bring it into existence.

After Calcination, what remains is then subjected to . . .

Square 2 – Dissolution

This is the process of further breaking down and transforming the conventional qualities of the mind. It occurs by taking something believed to be firm and stable (that which is left from step 1) and incorporating it into a liquid (connecting the two so to speak) so as to form a solution. In other words, what once was thought to be distinct and separate, is now obscured so that the course of the Universe can flow smoothly once more.

If Square 2 appears, the person for whom you are providing a reading has now moved from a new beginning and is about to be reborn. In order for this to happen, time must be taken for some introspection and quiet reflection in order to determine what is real and what is not.

Once this melting and softening occurs, we then proceed to . . .

Square 3 – Separation

This is the process whereby the result of the liquefaction activity is now scrutinized and separated out so as to encourage, tend, and care for one's authentic dreams and intentions. This is the place from which prized creation takes place as things and thoughts of inferior and peripheral status are set aside. This is the place from which the mother sets her child free to build their own life.

If Square 3 appears, the individual receiving the reading has now moved past introversion and contemplation and has set aside their own ego in order to determine what should be kept and what is truly indispensable.

Once that occurs, we move to . . .

Square 4 – Conjunction

This is the process of assembling a new substance or person by combining what was rescued and saved during the Separation. This is the building block, so to speak, of our true self and is comprised of evenly matched opposites that fortify and maintain what is to come. This is the place from which the monarch governs his kingdom.

If Square 4 appears in a reading, all the connecting – the coming together – has been completed and the construction of one's personal castle commences. This person is thus able to live under diverse situations.

After this co-existence is achieved, the following occurs . . .

Square 5 – Mortification

This is the process whereby our joined self is now allowed to decay or deteriorate. There is a lack of care and attention to the body of the substance as it is left to decompose. Indeed, this may also be thought of as a metaphorical act of dying and then restoration to life with a new energy and binding force. Fundamental change occurs at this stage with the delivering of higher knowledge or enlightenment through self-denial and discipline.

When Square 5 appears, the person receiving the reading is undergoing a type of extinguishing or extinction of a prior way of life and there is an "appearance" of the loss of power. However, this is a mere façade and a new ability and potential is discovered and restored.

With this elevated grasp of the world, we advance to . . .

Square 6 – Fermentation

This is the process of breaking down and reassembly of our newly born, higher self by adding tension. There are three main Fermentation methods: warm, cool, and what is called "wild" or "spontaneous" heat. This disquieting of and catalyst for the soul ultimately procures an energy – a higher passion and spiritedness – that unites us with those around us.

When Square 6 is present, the person receiving the reading is operating on a very deep and profound level. They have embraced – not only himself or herself – but are in the process of caressing, holding, and embodying those who are important in their life.

Once joined and coupled with the world, we are reduced, yet again, by . . .

Square 7 – Combustion

This is the process that greatly increases the power and value of the transformed substance through a burst of focused strength and drive. Combustion is an explosive attack or blast that results in a violent and sudden change in the way things were before. In the throes of this ignition – this release of light – there is pain. However, in the aftermath, the distress is followed by pleasure.

When Square 7 is present, the person receiving the reading is in the process of revealing and operating both their heat and their light. In other words, the person being read has energy on the rise and their actions are very visible at the moment.

The effects of this mechanism are then subjected to . . .

Square 8 – Distillation

This is the process of purification whereby the disrupted substance that has been derived from the Combustion method is now pressed and concentrated and filtered. It is the exercise of concentration, attentiveness, and single-mindedness. It is the ascent of one's life force by removing the material world and returning, once again, to the realm of consciousness and thought.

When Square 8 is present, the person being read is struggling against their material world and trying to implement their genuine and deep-seated self in its place. At the very least, they are operating from a higher level that seeks to restrain and curb the substance of life.

Having earned this lofty existence, we are, at last, treated to . . .

Square 9 – Coagulation

This is the final process – before we start all over again – wherein we change our substance from the wholesome and uncontaminated higher self or mind back into real, physical matter. This is the end that begs a new beginning. It is the need of the mind to have a viable and visible form in order to express itself. This process provides both a new lifetime and a continuation of creation. This is the culmination of the process needed for total transformation.

When Square 9 is present in a reading, the person being read is at the last stage of their current process. This individual's body and soul have been reinvented and joined together and a revitalization is taking place.

Not all of these processes will be present when you give a reading. In fact, you may find particular Places of Power are given emphasis out of their numerical order. This is normal and to be expected. In your readings, give emphasis to those squares that cry out to be noticed but also remark upon those missing squares that might need more attention. A missing process can be as important as a highlighted one for us to arrive at the final outcome. Likewise, no two people's order of processes will necessarily be the same. It is the unique order of doing things that makes us individuals.

PART FOURTEEN
THE VITRUVIAN TREE OF LIFE

According to the Kabbalah, in the beginning everything was God.

When God contracted to make room for creation,

spiritual energy filled the void. The energy poured into vessels

which strained to hold the great power. The vessels shattered,

sending countless shards, bits of the glowing matter,

into the vastness of the universe.

– Leonard Nimoy

In earlier chapters, you learned a vast collection of patterns to form when *The Vitruvian Square's* Power Places are combined. Now, I want to share with you one more of my favorites – The Tree of Life! There are actually two Tree of Life structures to bring to light – one situated along the Axis of Power, the other is along the Axis of Protection.

First, some brief background of how we're using The Tree of Life in conjunction with *The Vitruvian Square*. The mystical tradition known as the Kabbalah is, for most, an intricate explanation - often visual in nature - of the relationships between the Creator and Creation. At a fundamental level, the Kabbalah can be thought of as a set of teachings about the Nature of Everything. One of the orphic symbols used to express these concepts is known as The Tree of Life or Sacred Tree. The Tree is usually depicted with 10 nodes or spheres and 22 connecting lines. The spheres are generally arranged in three columns. At its most basic level, The Tree of Life is a diagram of the emanations and radiating matter from the Divine down to the material plane and then back up again.

Here is what the classic Tree of Life looks like.

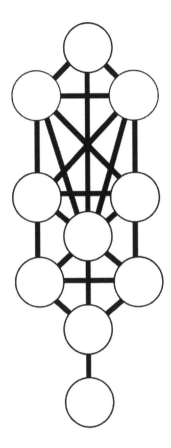

Figure 46 - Classic Tree of Life Configuration

The Seven Vitruvian Spheres

You can also take the usual Tree of Life and overlay it into *The Vitruvian Square* in two different directions. When you do so, you discover that seven Places of Power within *The Vitruvian Square* are highlighted.

The Tree of Life pattern that runs along the Axis of Power is made up of

Squares 1 (A, J, S), 2 (B, K, T), 4 (D, M, V), 5 (E, N, W), 6 (F, O, X), 8

(H, Q, Z), and 9 (I, R) (Squares 3 and 7 are not present).

1 AJS BEGINNING MAGICIAN WHEEL SUN	2 BKT CONNECTING H. PRIESTESS JUSTICE JUDGEMENT	3 CLU CREATING EMPRESS HANGED MAN WORLD
4 DMV BUILDING EMPEROR DEATH	5 ENW CHANGING HIEROPHANT TEMPERANCE	6 FOX UNITING LOVERS DEVIL
7 GPY DEFEATING CHARIOT TOWER	8 HQZ MOVING STRENGTH STAR	9 IR COMPLETING HERMIT MOON

Figure 47 - Tree of Life Axis of Power Tree of Life

When you choose to do a reading with *The Vitruvian Square* and

this Axis of Power configuration appears, you have a situation where the

acts of creating and destroying are absent, and the focus is more on

moving forward and finishing what was started. Because of the presence of Square 1 and the absence of Square 3, this is a pattern that addresses

outcomes more than obligations.

The Tree of Life pattern that runs along the Axis of Protection is

made up of the consecutive Squares 2 (B, K, T), 3 (C, L, U), 4 (D, M, V),

5 (E, N, W), 6 (F, O, X), 7 (G, P, Y), and 8 (H, Q, Z) (Squares 1 and 9

are not present).

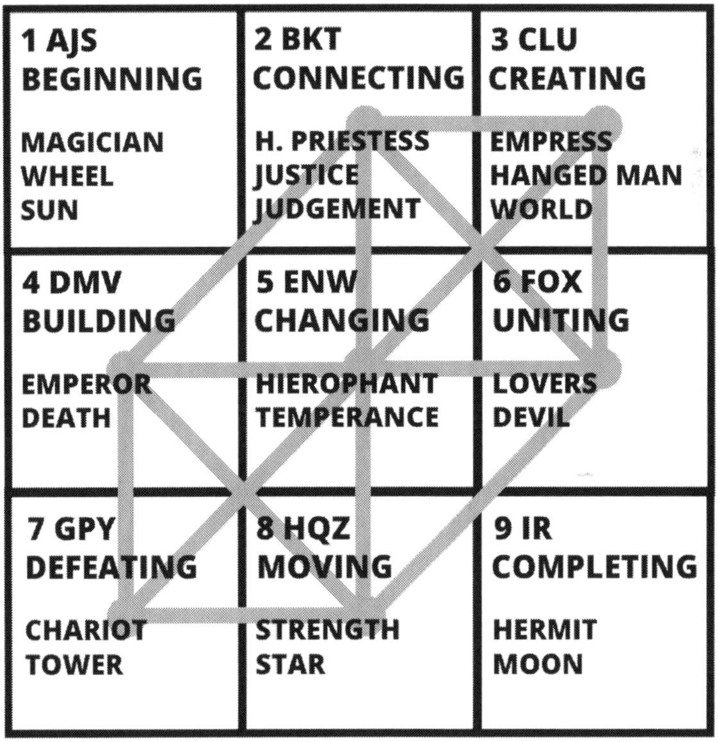

Figure 48 - Tree of Life Axis of Protection Tree of Life

When this Axis of Protection arrangement exists, you have a setting where the focus is on producing, generating, and bringing something into being. This is also all about the celebration of triumph for such an act of creation. However, notably absent from this pattern are the actual deeds of starting and finishing the project or idea. Because of the presence of Square 3 and the absence of Square 1, this is a pattern that addresses responsibilities more than consequences.

You can see that both patterns start in the Plane of Thought and, naturally enough, end in the Plane of Action. Both patterns, rightly, share the entire Plane of Passion.

This is merely the beginning of what can be found when applying Kabbalistic thinking to *The Vitruvian Square*. Naturally, The Tree of Life emulates the Kabbalah's *Etz haChayim* (Tree of Life). This ancient role model is an ancient design intended, among other more sublime uses, to show both the act and the path of Creation. I wonder if you can now see that the Tree of Life patterns are representations of the Universe – treasure maps, if you will – and that they epitomize the concept of As Above, So Below.

In comparison, the *Etz haChayim*, in most depictions, has ten spaces (or Sephirot). Our Tree of Life is a symbolic shape and reminder of the *Etz haChayim's* deep-rooted concepts. In other words, when the Tree of Life appears in a *Vitruvian Square* reading, it speaks of the origin of your world and your place in it.

I encourage you to make more discoveries as to the comparisons and resemblance of the Kabbalah and *The Vitruvian Square*. I think you will be delighted to find the parallels that exist and that can be put into use by you in your readings.

The Three Pillars

Overlaid onto this iconic symbol, there are usually further images that depict what are known as the Four Worlds and the Three Pillars. I will leave a deeper discussion of the Four Worlds for a later time. Right now, I want to discuss the Three Pillars; a concept that will provide you with some ample meditation practice.

The Three Pillars are distinguished by the following themes: Severity, Mercy, and Balance. You might also think of these as Intensity or Fierceness, Grace or Tolerance, and Symmetry or Equality, respectively. It should be no surprise to discover that the same Pillars exist within *The Vitruvian Square*!

In *The Vitruvian Square* matrix, the Pillar of Severity is located on the right-hand side of the image (or the left side as you face the illustration). The Pillar is made up of Squares 1, 4, and 7. These squares make up a literal tower of strength and intensity. It is a masculine (sweeping, dynamic, and practical) force to be reckoned with, but can be menacing if not controlled. This is also called the Plane of Outcomes and deals with choices and consequences. Intentions, goals, and ambitions are sustained in this column. Here you will find a sense of purpose.

The Pillar of Mercy is located on the left-hand side of our image (or the right side as you face the illustration). This Pillar is made up of Squares 3, 6, and 9. These squares make up a tower of compassion and tolerance. It is a feminine (pliable, gentle, and fluid) force that seeks to give goodness, but can be too kind at times. This is also called the Plane of Duty and controls our memories and feelings of responsibility. Passion, love, and desire all live here. But, so does one's temper.

Finally, the Pillar of Balance is the constant that exists in *The Vitruvian Square*. It is the middle column and is made up of Squares 2, 5, and 8. This is where fairness, steadiness, and symmetry are found. It is a neutral force that is constantly giving and taking from the two adjacent pillars and so must constantly stabilize itself. In *The Vitruvian Square* system, this is also called the Plane of Values; the place where our opinions and beliefs are housed. This is the place where you find staying

power, commitment, and endurance.

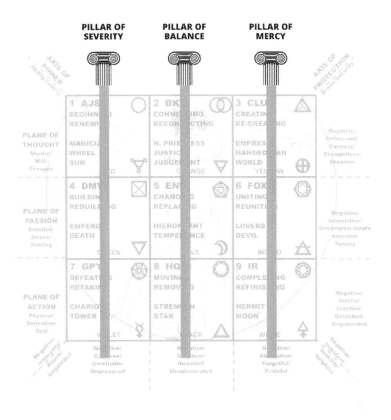

Figure 49 - The Vitruvian Square Three Pillars

A little contemplation of the three different Pillars will reveal that

the specific squares that make-up each of them all share comparable

features and traits. However, you will also find how each Pillar supports

and requires the other to be complete. Once you make those general

associations, start to meditate upon the individual characteristics of each

Pillar's Places of Power (the squares that make up each Pillar) and start to scrutinize the qualities of each one in relation to its designated Pillar.

Most importantly, as you delve deeper into *The Vitruvian Square* you become aware that none of the Places of Power are to be viewed solely in isolation and that all have their dual aspects that keep them in perfect balance. The concept of a trinity exists in many cultures and beliefs. See how many different trinities you can find hidden within *The Vitruvian Square* matrix (not just the Pillars, themselves, but amongst the various squares, planes, and axes).

The Four Realms

As you have seen, there are Three Pillars that exist within *The Vitruvian Square*; the Kabbalistic trinity that is said to be comprised of three hidden lights or columns. Now, we turn our attention to the related concept of The Four Realms. In the Kabbalah, The Four Realms represent, among other things, the four stages of formation of the Universe. These four instants in time can be thought of like this:

STAGE ONE: The Guiding Light. This is the bright idea or inspiration that is the catalyst for everything that follows. This is the realm of the infinite. Kabbalistic Association: Atzilut (emanated from). Element: Fire

STAGE TWO: The Invention. This is the expansion of creativity into a actual creative brainchild. This is where nothing becomes something. Kabbalistic Association: Briyah (creation). Element: Air

STAGE THREE: The Passion. This is where desire and enthusiasm impel an invention into a solid plan. It is here that intention is made into a substantial blueprint for success. Kabbalistic Association: Yetzira (formation). Element: Water

STAGE FOUR: The Building. This is the point at which creation is made complete and real. And, the creation, itself, takes on its own independence. Kabbalistic Association: Asiyah (action). Element: Earth

Applied to *The Vitruvian Square*, these four Realms of Creation appear, as follows:

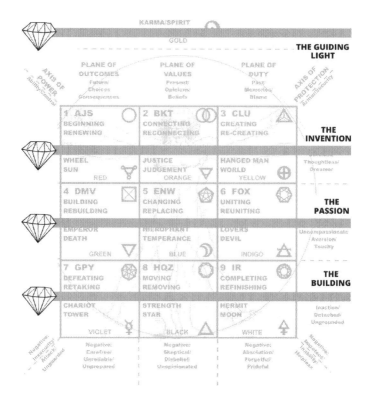

Figure 50 - The Vitruvian Square Four Realms

The four Realms of Creation can be used to review any creative project in which you are engaged. In other words, you can use *The Vitruvian Square* as a way to visualize or conceptualize any stage of a creative process. By going deeper, you can then use the various Places of Power within the matrix to determine what might be emphasized or missing at any given time.

As with the Three Pillars, the Realms of Creation are not to be viewed in complete isolation from each other. Rather, I recommend that you think of the boundaries of each realm as the place where one river runs into another; their powerful waters coming together, mixing, and creating a new current in the process.

The Realms of Creation, by the way, do not just depict a top-down view of life (from inspiration to culminating action). Indeed, the Realms of Creation can also be a top-up view (finding one's self in the world and aspiring for more).

Vitruvian Tree of Life Meditation

Finally, each one of the Places of Power within *The Vitruvian Square* can be used as a meditation jumping-off point. You can take each numbered square and contemplate how it interacts with its own Realm of Creation, the Realm of Creation just above it, and the one just below it. Bear in mind that *The Vitruvian Square* and the Kabbalah's Tree of Life are essentially circular in nature (they form a loop of sorts). Thus, from Place of Power 0 you would contemplate the realm of Invention as emanating downward from it, and the realm of action being above and giving life to Place of Power 0. With a little thought, you will easily begin to realize the Kabbalistic concept of As Above, So Below in every aspect of *The Vitruvian Square*.

I offer all of this for you to easily recognize that the Universe is multi-layered and in a constant fluid state. These continued changes and fluctuations can be used by you to help create the life you want to live and to explain why certain things have occurred when, where, and as they did.

PART FIFTEEN
THE I CHING AND PRINCIPLES OF REALITY

The I Ching insists upon self-knowledge throughout.

The method by which this is to be achieved is open to every kind of misuse,

and is therefore not for the frivolous-minded and immature;

nor is it for intellectualists and rationalists.

It is appropriate only for thoughtful and reflective people

who like to think about what they do and what happens to them.

– Carl Jung

The Vitruvian Square owes part of its origin to the Lo Shu Square.

Naturally, I have been asked how *The Vitruvian Square*, the I Ching, and

the Bagua correspond with each other. For those who might not already know, ancient Chinese legend tells of a great flood that occurred in pre-

historic times. Following the deluge, a remarkable turtle came out of the

water; the back of its shell containing a discernible arrangement of dots.

These dots became known as the Lo Shu pattern and presupposed a

three-by-three grid of numbers/meanings/associations.

Some claim that the three-by-three grid housed eight meaningful

trigrams; each trigram made up of broken and unbroken lines. The eight

trigrams constitute some fundamental principles of reality for the Taoist

and are often called the Bagua. The Bagua is commonly associated with

the Lo Shu square. It is only natural to show you how the 8 trigrams fit

into *The Vitruvian Square* matrix, and to easily demonstrate how energy

flows between the squares.

1 = ☵ = Water = Endless

2 = ☷ = Earth = Receptive

3 = ☳ = Thunder = Shaking

4 = ☴ = Wind = Grounding

5 = Yin Yang

6 = ☰ = Heaven = Forceful

7 = ☱ = Lake = Unlocked

$8 = \ \Xi\Xi \ = $ Mountain = Bound

$9 = \ \Xi\Xi \ = $ Fire = Radiant

An expanded version of this with some basic correspondences from Lo Shu, I Ching, and Bagua theories would look like this when superimposed upon *The Vitruvian Square*:

Position 5, you notice, does not host a trigram. Rather, it represents the wonderful Ying Yang concept; the Place of Power where perceived extremes and the trivial, opposing forces and those which are aligned, and differences and similarities all come together, and then give rise to each other all over again. This is where the ebb and flow of spirited reality takes place.

One more thing . . . you can combine the individual Places of Power within *The Vitruvian Square* to create sixty-four of the same types of hexagram fusions as you find with the Bagua and I Ching systems of divination. In the classic I Ching, these are 64 pairs of the basic 8 trigrams. For example, the hexagram for Youthful Folly is a combination of the inner, bottom trigram ☵ (Square 1 = Water = Endless) and outer, top trigram ☶ (Square 8= Mountain = Bound). Can you see how the concept of "Youthful Folly" is epitomized by The (inner) Fool and betrayed by (outer lack of) Strength?

Here's another example. If you double Square 6 (Heaven = Forceful) so that the trigram ☰ is both the inner, bottom character and the outer, top character, you have what is called "Creative Power." Creative Power is precisely what you get when you double the inspiration, energy, and desire of The Lovers.

Here's one more example so that you can see how you can play with this. If you combine ☳ (Square 3 =Thunder = Shaking) as the inner, bottom character with ☰ (Square 6 = Heaven = Forceful) as the outer, upper character you have what is called "Innocence." This is an apt way to describe what happens when you unite The Empress (Square 3) with The Lovers (Square 6).

Have fun exploring and meditating upon the sixty-four different hexagrams by combining the Places of Power from *The Vitruvian Square*. You'll soon discover the additional depth that exists within the matrix.

PART SIXTEEN
THE RULE OF THIRDS

You can observe a lot just by looking around.

– Yogi Berra

Have you ever reached a point in your readings where they stopped

flowing as easily as they used to?

Have you started to feel trapped in your interpretations or

reading style?

Are you bored with your oracle technique?

Just want something new?

This chapter was made for you!

Those of you who are familiar with photography may have heard of The Rule of Thirds; a kind of work-of-art, compositional and general rule of thumb. Simply, it involves the concept that you conjure up an image that is broken down into thirds (both horizontally and vertically) so that you have nine equal parts that are made distinct by the use of two equally-spaced horizontal lines and two equally-spaced vertical lines. Further, as John Thomas Smith said in his Remarks on Rural Scenery, . . .

And to give the utmost force and solidity to your work, some part of the picture should be as light, and some as dark as possible : These two extremes are then to be harmonized and reconciled to each other.

It is no accident that *The Vitruvian Square* has the same dominant structure and visual impact. Let's begin to explore why The Rule of Thirds used with *The Vitruvian Square* will yield such solid and compelling results for you.

Notice that there is a power grid of sorts built within the matrix structure.

There are four Lines of Consequence (two vertical and two horizontal lines).

Figure 51 - Lines of Consequence

Each of the four Lines of Consequence, in turn, serve as incredible and valuable distinctions, and a means to keep apart the various mental, emotional, and material worlds, as well as the several timings built into *The Vitruvian Square* (e.g., Past, Present, and Future).

Each Line of Consequence, on its own, can be thought of as either that which you are constantly drawing (e.g., your line in the sand) or that which is constantly being crossed. In other words, each Line of Consequence represents a repercussion, a ramification, or a principle. It is either that symbolic point where no further advance can or will be made by you, or it is that line that, once crossed, results in what you believe will be irrevocable changes. Our Lines of Consequence, then, are essentially the passionate parameters we use to box ourselves in and create boundaries. To put it another way, the various Lines of Consequence firmly signal the heartfelt divisions we create in our lives; an enthusiastic parceling out, if you will, of the way we allocate the various aspects of our being. It is no wonder, then, that these Lines of Consequence can so easily be used in a reading; either by themselves or as a complement to your use of the basic *Vitruvian Square* layout.

Further, the intersection of any two Lines of Consequence creates a Power Point. There are also four primary four-way intersections (the four corners of the Number 5 square).

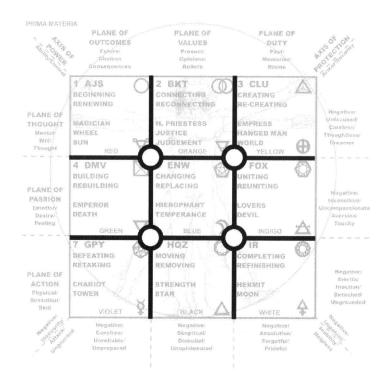

Figure 52 - The Power Points

Each of the four primary intersections (Power Points) of *The Vitruvian Square* that are created by the Lines of Consequence are situations of importance in a reading.

The first Power Point is made up of the intersection of the following Places of Power:

Square 1 (Beginning)

Square 2 (Connecting)

Square 4 (Building)

Square 5 (Changing)

When this Power Point is involved in a reading (in other words, one of more of your cards or oracle tools is touching this point because the card falls in Squares 1, 2, 4, or 5), there is an underlying indication – almost a subconscious guide – that new associations and interdependence are increasing, with a resulting change in a current situation. This is the Power Point of reshaping bonds by adding new friends and moving towards more structure to your life. As with all the Power Points, the more cards that are touching this location, the stronger that particular indication. Naturally, each indicator should be read in the context of its specific Place of Power.

The second Power Point is made up of the intersection of the following Places of Power:

Square 2 (Connecting)

Square 3 (Creating)

Square 5 (Changing)

Square 6 (Uniting)

When this Power Point is involved in a reading, there is an indication that new achievements and intellectual pursuits are coming, with a resulting change in a current situation. This is the Power Point of choosing to create change through binding and linking yourself with others and a move towards a desired outcome in the world around you. The more cards that direct you to this spot, the more you are joining forces – internally and externally – with others.

The third Power Point is made up of the intersection of the following Places of Power:

Square 4 (Building)

Square 5 (Changing)

Square 7 (Defeating)

Square 8 (Moving)

When this Power Point is involved in a reading, there is an indication that the person being read has an emotional need and want to move away from the current situation. These choices, by the way, result from a desire to conquer a fear or vanquish a current, unwanted situation.

The fourth and final Power Point is made up of the intersection of the following Places of Power:

Square 5 (Changing)

Square 6 (Uniting)

Square 8 (Moving)

Square 9 (Completing)

When this Power Point is involved in a reading, there is an indication that the person being read is, like the last Power Point, moving away from a current situation. This time, however, the choice for change is provoked by the transforming of relationships in one's life at the moment. This is a Power Point of reacting to the ebb and flow of other people's energies.

In using *The Vitruvian Square* with the Rule of Thirds, more excitement, vitality, and fascination can be created in a reading by including an interpretation of the patterns and intersections that are seen. You look for and interpret the dynamic tension involved in your reading (in addition to the other elements you are used to reading). If you haven't noticed, yet, applying the Rule of Thirds to *The Vitruvian Square* is less about where the cards or other oracle device actually land or are placed (although those are important), and more about where you aim your attention.

One of the simplest ways to use all of this is to give a four-card reading by placing four cards (or other oracle items) on the four Situations of Importance. You then read just those four cards in the context of the Lines of Consequence and Power Points. One of the first things to notice is any particular Line of Consequence that stands out to you either through the overall theme of what the cards tell you or through intuition. Once a Line of Consequence draws your attention, think of it as something the person you are reading allows others to cross or consider whether this signifies how others are perceived as acting in a way that is not socially, emotionally, nor logically acceptable to the person being read.

In addition to doing a reading using only the Power Points (the four corners of the number 5 square), you can also lay out cards on *The Vitruvian Square* matrix in an intuitive, impromptu manner. Rather than strictly using the four corners, use whichever squares of the matrix that call to you. You can then look to see what Lines of Consequence are involved. In working in this fashion, look at *The Vitruvian Square* squares that are in play and start asking what each segment of a particular line means or represents. For example, there is a vertical segment running between Square 1 (Beginning) and Square 2 (Connecting). What line has to be crossed for someone to move between starting out with an idea and attaching something substantial to what, moments before, was only imaginary? If this segment of line is indicated in a reading (e.g., you have a card or cards in either Square 1 and/or Square 2), you can pull another card to decipher either what needs to happen to move this person from mere creativity to interdependence with the world around them (if they appear to be moving from Square 1 to Square 2) or what needs to happen to move this person from their bond with the world to more individuality (if they appear to be moving from Square 2 to Square 1). In using this segment of line, by the way, you will remember that it separates out the mental process that draws a distinction between the Future (The Plane of Outcomes) and the Present (The Plane of Values), and the difference between mentally focusing on outcomes and values (The Plane of Thought).

Another fun way to look at this handling is to ask yourself (using a card that appears in Square 1): What does The Magician have to do to become The High Priestess? Or (using a card that appears in Square 2), what does The High Priestess have to do to become The Magician? This type of exercise has been little used and certainly under-reported by others, and I want you to have this technique available to you now.

Let's look at another example. What if you wanted to interpret the segment that separates Square 4 (Building) and Square 7 (Defeating)? What can that division mean? Well . . . if we are going to progress from Square 4 to Square 7, we have to find what line must be crossed that will pull us from erecting a foundation to conquering something else. If we are moving from Square 7 to Square 4, conversely, we must find what will occur that will inspire us to change from a vanquishing mindset to one of improvement. You will also notice that we will be moving either from the material world (The Plane of Action) to the emotional world (The Plane of Passion) and vice versa.

Once again, you can also ask yourself (using a card that appears in Square 4): What does The Emperor have to do to become The Chariot? Or (using a card that appears in Square 7), what does The Chariot have to do to become The Emperor?

If you take the time to study each of the Lines of Consequence segment by segment, you will uncover many, many secrets about the way people approach their lives. Perhaps it's no coincidence at all that there are twelve different segments that comprise the Lines of Consequence. Indeed, the number 12 has great significance in the ancient world (for example, there were twelve principal gods of the Pantheon in Greece) and among the various religions (the Twelve Tribes of Israel, and the twelve days before Christmas, among others). Most juries are comprised of twelve layperson judges of the outside world. There are twelve signs of the Zodiac. And, when I work with people individually, I show them how there are twelve main categories of their life to consider and focus upon.

In addition to the four-card spread already discussed, you can also use the Lines of Consequence and the Power Points for a reading using sixteen cards (twelve cards for the line segments, and four cards for the points). Simply lay out the cards on the individual segments and points, rather than using the squares. You then read each segment and point and give your interpretation as to the energy and passion that needs to happen in order to move across the lines and from the points.

Of course, if you want a great meditation tool (and, yes, this too can be used for a reading), take any conjunction of four segments (for example, the segment between Square 1 and Square 2, the segment between Square 2 and Square 5, the segment between Square 5 and Square 4, and the segment between Square 5 and Square 1), and lay out one card for each segment and see what it tells you. After you consider this context, add a fifth card (the Power Point) to give a final lesson to be learned or energy to focus upon.

Enjoy this very rare and esoteric reading technique. I know it is a bit intricate. Be patient and work your way through the lines and points;

you will pleasantly find some added significance and, indeed, vitality in

your readings that were not present before.

PART SEVENTEEN
MISCELLANEOUS ODDS AND ENDS

The willing, Destiny guides them;

the unwilling, Destiny drags them.

- Seneca

Here is a collection of varied techniques and tools for use with your

Vitruvian Square readings.

Pendulums

If you don't know already, a pendulum is a divination tool that

has a weighted item on the end of a string or chain. For use with *The*

Vitruvian Square, either you or the person for whom you are reading hold

the pendulum over the real or imaginary square patterns on the reading surface (remember the imaginary or projected layout I mentioned earlier). As the pendulum is slowly moved about the layout, notice the areas over which it seems to be reacting. Alternatively, let the pendulum drop down and barely touch the tabletop's surface; the joining of the pendulum's tip with the surface being an indication of the locations or squares to be used. When the pendulum responds to various areas of *The Vitruvian Square*, make note of those locations, numbers and attributes to provide your reading.

Successes and Failures

There are times when an in-depth reading is neither needed nor desired. For those very quick and simple "yes-or-no" questions or "success-or-failure" type inquiries, use the following easily remembered rule:

ODD NUMBERS = YES

EVEN NUMBERS = NO

You can either use a single Place of Power to determine the answer or add the various locations/numbers together for one final sum.

Colors

Colors have long been known to have a visceral, deep-rooted impact on people. In case you want to add colors to your use of *The*

Vitruvian Square, this chart (Figure 53) will get you started:

0
GOLD

1 **RED**	**2** **ORANGE**	**3** **YELLOW**
4 **GREEN**	**5** **BLUE**	**6** **INDIGO**
7 **VIOLET**	**8** **BLACK**	**9** **WHITE**

Figure 53 - Color Attributes within The Vitruvian Square

You will note that the first seven squares – numbers 1 through 7 – are in "color of the rainbow" order. The easiest way to remember this order is to recall the curious name "ROY G. BIV" – Red, Orange, Yellow, Green, Blue, Indigo, and Violet. The last two squares (numbers 8 and 9) are Black and White; easy enough to remember as we use the phrase "black and white" not "white and black." If you need a further reminder, "B" comes before "W." Gold – that most precious metal – is also included for use with the number 0. Remember this by recalling that a "gold medal" means you came in first or "on top."

While not intended to be exhaustive, here are some attributes and meanings for you to apply to each of the colors:

Gold

Gold is the color of personal, spiritual, and karmic warmth. It is often described as "precious," "beautiful," and "brilliant." This is the color of abundance and success. It is also the color that represents achievement of the ultimate goal.

Red

Red, one of the primary colors, is the color of the Divine fire that burns within each soul. It is the color of desire and activity. Red brings with it intense emotions and cries out for attention. It is highly visible and can also represent courage while, at the same time, makes us stop and take notice.

Orange

Orange, a combination of Red and Yellow, is a color that represents taking the potential from the external world and stimulating it to form a new creation or idea. While this is a warm color, it is not as forceful as Red. Orange demands our attention but does so in a subtle way.

Yellow

Another primary color, Yellow is the color of the welcoming warmth of sunlight. This is the color of happiness, expansion, and expectation. It is also the symbol of hope, dreams, and wishes. Yellow "highlights" other things that are already in existence and cautions us to be careful, if necessary.

Green

Green is the combination of the primary colors Blue and Yellow. This is the color we most associate with Mother Nature, wildlife, and growing things. This is the color of things and people who are worldly, temporal, and cultivated. Green allows us to proceed forward safely. This is also the color most often associated with currency or money. As such, this is the color that represents resources, wealth, and undertakings.

Blue

Blue is one of the primary colors and represents tranquility and satisfaction. This is the color of water and the sky. As such, it represents emotions both high and low. Blue calms us down and is viewed as a symbol for devotion, piousness, and truthfulness. This is also the color of someone who is trustworthy and dependable.

Indigo

Indigo is created by combining the colors Blue and Red; more Blue than Red. You may know this color as "Royal Blue." This is the color of power and importance. Indigo represents the concept of service to others and having great affection and devotion. This is the color of the Mystic Union and creating a feeling of "Oneness."

Violet

Violet, too, is the combination of Blue and Red; this time with some White thrown in for good measure. This is the color of purpose, goals, and objectives; of determination and drive. Violet is also the color of inspiration and motivation. It is the color of focused energy to further a plan. Violet is a color that inspires and motivates.

Black

Black is the color of absolute boundaries. It is also the symbol for nothingness, extinction and rejection. It is the color of the night, shadows, and the mysteries the darkness brings. Black is elegant and affords perspective and depth to things. It is the color of status and fame. It is also the absence or lack of any other colors. Black sits in the background and makes everything else more visible.

White

White is the presence of all the colors at one time. It is a symbol of beginnings, freshness, and purity. White is the "start-over" color; a clean slate. It can also be the color of perfection. Like freshly fallen snow, it represents a freshness and exhilaration. There is an innocence and chasteness about White that leads us to believe it is otherworldly or not meant to stay pristine in this world for long.

Astrological Signs

For those of you with a starward bent, here is a chart (Figure 54) you might find interesting that provides the astrological correspondences to the nine squares (and the 0 location). I have used the Tarot Major Arcana as the bases for determining these symmetries. In all fairness, there is some debate as to the proper associations depending on which type of Tarot card deck you are using and one's particular background and grounding in Astrology. For that reason, there is some redundancy in the illustration that follows. Even if you don't agree with these particular correspondences, you will find the chart a stepping-stone for creating your own:

0 - AQUARIUS

1 GEMINI VIRGO SAGITTARIUS LEO	2 MOON LIBRA PLUTO	3 TAURUS LIBRA PISCES CAPRICORN
4 ARIES SCORPIO	5 TAURUS SAGITTARIUS	6 GEMINI CAPRICORN
7 CANCER MARS	8 LEO AQUARIUS	9 VIRGO PISCES

**Figure 54 - Astrological Attributes within
The Vitruvian Square**

What Your Subconscious Wants You To Know

In having performed thousands of readings for people, I have come to the conclusion that many times when a person asks a question there is a deeper insight that they want or need to know. This is not to discount or discourage a person from asking a specific question. However, there are certainly times when the question, itself, cries out for another question to be answered first.

In Part Nine of this book, I mentioned Sydney Omarr. In his wonderful 1950's book, "The Thought Dial" which appears to be based, at least in part, upon the 1920's book entitled "The Kabala of Numbers" by Sepharial, Omarr proposed providing a reading "without consciously thinking of a specific question." I have found, however, that allowing someone to think of a particular event, person, or question actually centers a reading and furnishes direction for a subconscious message.

Strengthening and expanding upon Omarr's and Sepharial's concepts, I always include a "This is what your Subconscious wants you to know" statement with my readings. While you can certainly use the original Omarr and Sepharial abstracts from their writings, I have found it much more fertile and precise to use the unique affirmations and commands from Figure 55.

To begin, have someone think of a question, an event, a specific time period, a person or a thing upon which they want your reading centered. Now you arrive at a specific Place of Power within *The Vitruvian Square* (using whichever of the numerous methods already given to arrive at a particular number). The square you have chosen or been shown now has the following messages for use with the person receiving the reading:

1	2	3
"Follow your creativity" "Tell a story" "Be accessible" "Be happy"	"Learn secrets" "Show mercy" "Remember"	"Give comfort and protection" "Hold to your possessions"
4	**5**	**6**
"Pursue your desires" "Be unforgettable" "Karma"	"Know your fears" "Concede" "Seek alchemy"	"Stay loyal to those you love" "Set some voluntary limits"
7	**8**	**9**
"Use your anger" "Show some self-restraint" "Disruption comes naturally"	"Think things over" "Have courage" "Be filled with promise"	"Walk away" "Use the past to help you" "Be filled with wonder"

Figure 55 - "What Your Subconscious Wants You to Know"

As you can see, there are various messages for use with each number. Depending on the person being read and what your intuition tells you at the time of a reading, choose the specific message that seem appropriate to you. My intent in providing you more than one message per square is to give you variety. Don't just read. Use each and every message without giving thought to how congruent it feels at the moment.

Of Things Lost

In closing out this chapter, here is a fun technique to use at the appropriate time. Sepharial noted in his "The Kabala of Numbers" that the use of numbers may extend "to a practically unlimited variety of affairs." He went on to provide a numerological basis for finding lost objects. With some minor revisions to update the material for modern use, here is Sepharial's analysis adapted for *The Vitruvian Square* (Figure 56). As Sepharial noted in his original offering, the providing of specific information for lost items is "remarkable."

1	2	3
- Main part of the house - Living room - Bedroom near white linen	- In the house - In or near a vase or bowl - Someone will help find	- In a passage - Between papers - Where men congregate
4	**5**	**6**
- The item is not lost - It's in your possession	- Under/near headwear - It will be found when you stop looking	- Near footwear - On a shelf or stand
7	**8**	**9**
- The item will not be found - Deceit is involved -Ask someone	- Found on a shelf/ledge - In a field - Connected to illness	- It is with a child - May have been lost in a quarrel

Figure 56 - Sepharial's "Of Things Lost" Applied to The Vitruvian Square

In using Figure 56, have someone think of an object they fear lost or misplaced. As before, you determine a specific number within *The Vitruvian Square*. The number decided upon has a fastidious importance for your further use.

PART EIGHTEEN
PALMISTRY

As for the future, your task is not to foresee it, but to enable it.

- Antoine de Saint-Exupery

Irrespective of the form of divination that you find most comfortable and natural, there can be no denying that palmistry holds a fascination and charm for everyone. After all, we carry our hands around with us. All you need to do is mention that you know palm reading and watch the hands that are thrust before you. It is only fitting, then, that I show you a way to use *The Vitruvian Square* in a palmistry setting. Please note that by slightly modifying the handling, you can use the following technique for use with any reading art that utilizes the study of the shapes and placement of symbols/figures/marks on the body.

Figure 57 shows *The Vitruvian Square* applied to the left hand,

only. I don't think using *The Vitruvian Square* in its "normal" orientation

corresponds correctly when applied to the right hand. As such, to enjoy

The Vitruvian Square with the right hand you simply reverse the placement

of everything. By now, this should be a comfortable mental exercise for

you to accomplish.

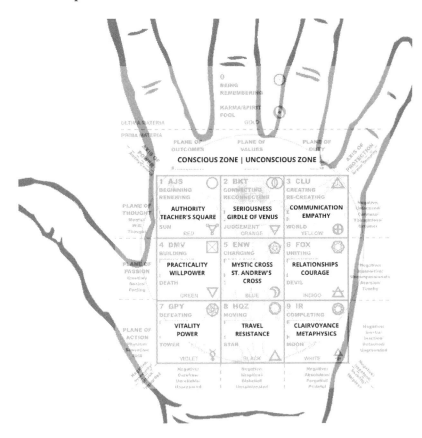

Figure 57 - Palmistry within The Vitruvian Square

There are some bolded items in Figure 57. These are the areas that apply specifically to palmistry and would be those items that might appear on a person's palm when reading it. You will also note that the four vertical lines that partially outline *The Vitruvian Square* correspond to the four fingers when extended upward. The thumb would be on the side.

The challenge is having the Heart and Head lines generally appearing in the planes of thought and passion, respectively. On first blush, this appears counter-intuitive. However, on closer testing, you will find that these lines of the hand actually bolster and underscore their affiliated planes. For example, the configuration and direction/orientation of the Heart line within the Plane of Thought would demonstrate how the two act together.

Generally, the Heart line, continuing with my example, originates in square 3 (creating - The Empress) moves into square 2 (connecting - The High Priestess) and may encroach into square 1 (beginning - The Magician). The depth and angle of the line would certainly give you much to speak about. I think the fact that the Heart line grows from the "creating" square is quite suitable for a discussion of how emotion is necessary for any great work of creation to take place.

The Head line, in turn, originates in square 4 (building - The Emperor). It will broadly sweep across square 5 (changing - The Hierophant) and then may turn down towards squares 8 (moving - Strength) or 7 (defeating - The Chariot). Yet again, I find these squares congruent with an extended exchange about how one's "head" affects these various areas.

The Fate line will generally run through squares 2, 5, 8 - originating in square 2. It may break apart in square 5 (which is consistent with a discussion of change). It may curve as it reaches square 8 and, in fact, terminate before then.

In giving a reading combining palms and *The Vitruvian Square*, I find it helpful to discuss the "conscious" and "unconscious" zones of the hand. The conscious zones (those areas that deal with intent, knowing and conceiving) are represented fully by squares 1 (The Magician), 4 (The Emperor), and 7 (The Chariot). The unconscious zones (those areas that are part of the mind where thoughts and actions take place and which the person might otherwise be unaware) are exemplified by squares 3 (The Empress), 6 (The Lovers), and 9 (The Hermit). Squares 2 (The High Priestess), 5 (The Hierophant), and 8 (Strength) have both feet firmly planted in both zones.

PART NINETEEN
ADDITIONAL TOOLS

Here is a collection of additional thoughts, concepts, and notions for use

with *The Vitruvian Square* that, quite frankly, don't fall into the category of

divination but which work wonderfully well. Most importantly, these

supplemental approaches yield you the ability to set whatever tone you

might want to the reading experience. Many people bring their own

beliefs and faith to a reading. Once you determine their convictions

and/or openness, use any of the following items to bring a deeper sense

of meaning to the experience.

SIGILS

Logic only gives a man what he needs;

Magic gives him what he wants.

- Tom Robbins

The word "sigil" comes from either the Roman and Old English term, *Sigillium*, meaning "seal" or the Hebrew word, *Segulah*, meaning "a word, action or item of spiritual action." A sigil is essentially an allegorical symbol – an emotionally charged icon, if you will – created to provide the bearer with a particular meaning or intent and power. I will not go into the specific "magic" that can be worked with sigils. There are any number of books and information available should you seek to explore the fascinating word of spellcasting and practical magic on your own.

For those times when it would benefit the person you are reading for whatever reason, to have something concrete to take away from their time with you, you can use *The Vitruvian Square* to generate a personal sigil or seal based on the patterns you discover during the reading. This magical drawing, then, would be based on the numerical significance and/or sequence in a particular name.

Using the name, "RICHARD DRACO," from our previous

example, the sigil would be (Figure 58):

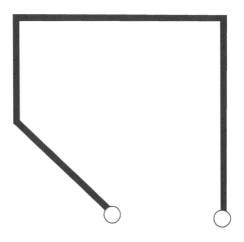

Figure 58 - The Name, "Richard Draco," as a Sigil

To arrive at Figure 58, you first break down the name,

"RICHARD DRACO," into its numerological components. "RICHARD

DRACO" would equate to R = 9, I = 9, C = 3, H = 8, A = 1, R = 9, D

= 4, D = 4, R = 9, A = 1, C = 3, and O = 6. The numbers plotted on

The Vitruvian Square would look like this (Figure 59):

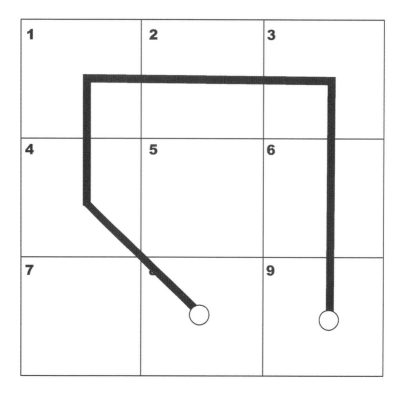

Figure 59 - "Richard Draco" Plotted on The Vitruvian Square

In plotting the numbers, you will see the large collection of 9's. That is our starting point and, thus, I place a circle as the starting point. I place another circle at the ending point. If there are two or more numbers that are highly indicated, I may place more than one circle within the sigil, itself.

Once all numbers are marked, simply look at the squares that are active and create a pattern or symbol that seems most logical to you. It is very similar to the old game of "connect the dots." You may have several options available – go with your gut! There is no wrong answer here. You are creating a powerful and personal symbol to represent your time together with the person for whom you are reading.

Incantations (and Affirmations)

First say to yourself what you would be;

and then do what you have to do.

- Epictetus

Words can well be used to conjure a sought-after effect, feeling, or event. When coupled with an emotion, the recitation is mighty and wondrous. Incantations, of course, involve the practice of saying or observing (in this case) words to call up a magical outcome. The use of this type of ritual is much more than simply asserting or stating the apparent or wanted truthfulness of something. Rather, the use of incantations involves actually calling up the correct mix of desires, expectations, and beliefs to achieve a wanted consequence.

Most importantly, the following tool focuses the incantation and occupies the mind so that you think of little else. Whether used for your own personal ends or fashioned by you so that it can be used by someone else, this is, without a doubt, quite a powerful and potent process. The use of *The Vitruvian Square* to create and enhance incantations and affirmations for an individual actually provides you the ability to begin to fashion and shape a person's entire cause-and-effect method of dealing with life - essentially a more detailed, master plan, if not a simple acknowledgment – of their life strategies. By generating a personal incantation, you are able to help someone decide, in advance, how decisions and choices will be made.

To use *The Vitruvian Square's* nine Places of Power for this process, you will import the various aspects of each "place" to the individual words of your chosen incantation. Although it is likely very obvious to you, I must remind you that, in designing an incantation for use with this stratagem you use only nine words! For example, an ancient expression I use and which life coach and motivational teacher, Anthony Robbins, is fond of exhorting is: "All the [fill in your desired emotion/attribute/skill] I need is within me now!" Here is how those words (in bold) would be set in the nine Places of Power (Figure 60):

1 AJS	2 BKT	3 CLU
BEGINNING	CONNECTING	CREATING
ALL	**THE**	**[FILL IN]**
MAGICIAN	H. PRIESTESS	EMPRESS
WHEEL	JUSTICE	HANGED MAN
SUN	JUDGEMENT	WORLD
4 DMV	5 ENW	6 FOX
BUILDING	CHANGING	UNITING
I	**NEED**	**IS**
EMPEROR	HIEROPHANT	LOVERS
DEATH	TEMPERANCE	DEVIL
7 GPY	8 HQZ	9 IR
DEFEATING	MOVING	COMPLETING
WITHIN	**ME**	**NOW**
CHARIOT	STRENGTH	HERMIT
TOWER	STAR	MOON

Figure 60 - Incantation Plotted on The Vitruvian Square

Let's examine how the combination of the placement of these words within *The Vitruvian Square* strengthens and endows the incantation, itself. First, look at the bolded words (the incantation, itself) and then notice and appreciate their collocation with the natural attributes of the nine places of *The Vitruvian Square*. You will be taking the incantation and meditating upon each individual word and its place within *The Vitruvian Square* world. Through such reflection, you actually give more internal power and meaning to your selected words.

Using my example, above, then, you might think of the following in meditating and using the incantation. Please note that I have only focused on the Tarot in this particular analysis. Any of the numerous dimensions of the various squares already discussed in this book may be used with equal impact.

Square 1 - ALL

This is the "whole thing" - what is the greatest and most possible of everything - the investing of your whole interest or energy in something. How appropriate that the word "ALL" is contained within the Magician, the Wheel of Fortune, and the Sun's collective place of power. Each one of these Major Arcana archetypes represents, with their varied nuances, the concept of being completely given or fully absorbed.

Square 2 - THE

The word "the" is used as a marker or distinguishing symbol in our language. It provides a specific or refined effect to the words around it. Moreover, it is possessive in nature. Note the similarity of those constructs with the High Priestess, Justice, and Judgement.

Square 3 - [YOUR CHOSEN WORD]

The word you choose here is limited only by your own imagination and need. For example, you might insert any of the following - love, joy, courage, knowledge, skill, hope, humility, etc. How fortunate we are to now find that the very emotion, skill, and aid you want to invoke is in the place of power of the Empress, the Hanged Man and the World! This is truly the space of creating.

Square 4 - I

The word "I" makes reference to the narrator of the story (e.g, "you"). It is a symbolic word of independence, stability, and might. Note how those are the very dimensions of the Emperor and Death.

Square 5 - NEED

This particular word sets forth the condition of the entire incantation; the requirement that has caused the ritual to be started in the first place. In other words, if you didn't feel you "needed" to call forth the power of the word located in Square 3 you wouldn't be playing with this to begin with. The word "need" means that something is a requirement and an obligation. Take time to notice and appreciate how those attributes are shared by the Hierophant and Temperance.

Square 6 - IS

"Is" means to exist or to live. It relates to the sense of belonging to something or someone. And it infers the idea of growth and "becoming." So, too, are these concepts underscored by the Lovers and the Devil.

Square 7 - WITHIN

This word conveys the notion that all is "in" your mind, heart, or spirit. Something is "within" when it is "inside." The Charioteer, to be truly deserving of victory and in order to hold up under the spoils of his efforts, must have first resolved in his mind, heart and spirit the motives for his actions and beliefs. The Tower reminds us that, unless we are stalwart on the inside, we can be broken from the outside.

Square 8 - ME

"Me" is the objective case form of the word "I" (Square 4). This refers to "himself" or "herself." Look and you will see that this is placed in the square also occupied by Strength and the Star; cards that also exemplify non-subjective goals to be attained.

Square 9 - NOW

The word "now" means "at the present time." It is a word of immediacy and cries out for something to happen without delay. Aren't those the very attributes of the Hermit and Moon? With both of these Arcana, they reflect what is happening around them "now." In the case of the Hermit, he is removed from the world yet ponders and muses and shines from the very creation from which he believes he is isolated. Similarly, the Moon does not glow on its own.

With this particular example, I have set forth an incantation that assists you or the person getting the reading in calling forth an attribute, feeling, or skill you might otherwise think you are lacking. You can also use this formula to ruminate over incantations such as the mystical saying, "Thine is the Kingdom, power and glory forever, Amen." This would be plotted onto *The Vitruvian Square* as:

Thine (Square 1) is (Square 2) the (Square 3) Kingdom (Square 4), power (Square 5) and (Square 6) glory (Square 7) forever, (Square 8) Amen (Square 9).

Clearing, Cleansing & Balancing

It should be no surprise that *The Vitruvian Square* can be used for an energy clearing/cleansing ceremony. Let me share the process so you can instantly and easily use this terrific way to feel better and be more focused.

Using *The Vitruvian Square* matrix, bring your attention to the nine squares that make up the primary matrix (Numbers 1 through 9). Number 0, as you know, is at the very top. We will be using all ten locations for our clearing/cleansing strategy.

STEP 1: Sit comfortably in a chair or restfully lie down. Take a few deep, freeing breaths, and close your eyes.

STEP 2: Visualize the overall structure of *The Vitruvian Square* and its nine distinct Places of Power locations (Squares 1 through 9). You don't need to have the correspondences for each square memorized as you will be referring back to this book at Step 11. Bring the three squares at the top, three squares in the middle, and three squares at the bottom clearly into the focus of your mind's eye. Continue breathing deeply as you begin to notice that each of *The Vitruvian Square* positions is filling with bright, white light.

STEP 3: Bring your inner vision to focus on Square Number 1. See that square infused with white light. As you breathe in and out, the light almost seems to pulse with your breath.

STEP 4: Shift your inner vision to focus on Square Number 2. Now, see Square Number 2 infused with its own white light. This square, too, seems to have a rhythm of its own . . . yet, it is in tune with your own, deep breathing.

STEP 5: Continue advancing your inner vision to each of the remaining seven squares (Square Numbers 3 through 9). Each time you use your imagination to a new square, fill that square with white light and notice its throbbing brilliance.

STEP 6: When you have finished paying attention to each of the individual nine Places of Power, widen your inner vision so that you are now seeing all nine squares at one time – as if your inner camera has moved from a close-up of each square to a wider, larger, all-inclusive establishing shot of the full matrix. See *The Vitruvian Square*, in its entirety, lit up with white light; the glow of each square touching on and spreading to each of its neighbors.

STEP 7: Now, start to notice whether there are any dark areas in your personal *Vitruvian Square*; areas that feel gloomy, or unlit, or dingy. When you discover such places, make a mental note of which numbered squares are impacted (we'll use them later). For each shadowy area, narrow your attention, once more. Using your inner vision, begin to purposefully fill any dark areas you have noticed with white light until the darkness is obliterated.

STEP 8: Finally, widen your inner vision and zoom out one last time until you can see the entire *Vitruvian Square*, yet again. You begin to notice, for the first time, that there is a ball of light above the nine squares (at the Number 0) position. This ball of light is so bright and so powerful that it is sending rays of light into the nine squares below it. Just take all of this in and experience how you feel.

STEP 9: Open your eyes and finish with some more cleansing breaths.

STEP 10: Take a few moments and notice how you feel now, compared with how you felt when you first started this technique. Are you more relaxed or full of energy? Are you more focused or more aware?

STEP 11: Go back to *The Vitruvian Square* image in the book and find the correspondences/meanings for the areas that you noticed were dark and gloomy. These are areas that needed your focus and which you have now cleared and bolstered and reinforced. Be sensitive to any internal messages that these squares and their meanings hold for you; knowing that, by clearing them with white light, you have added new balance to your inner harmony.

PART TWENTY
THE VITRUVIAN PALACE – AN INNER JOURNEY

Nowhere can man find a quieter

or more untroubled retreat than in his own soul.

- Marcus Aurelius

Pathworking with Tarot cards is a time-honored visualization and magical technique. Simply, you take an individual Major Arcana card, study the card's images, and then close your eyes and imagine yourself inside the card. For example, you might use a particular card as a doorway, or a window, or a painting to launch your inner vision and creativeness. Once you bring the scene/card to life, you then allow events to unfold – remembering the symbols, wisdom, and insights that are gifted to you.

Upon returning from this inner journey, you write everything down for later review and contemplation. There are as many ways to perform pathworking as there are individuals. Indeed, some routines are highly complicated. Others are simple and straightforward.

It is exciting to discover that *The Vitruvian Square* can be used in a similar way. First, imagine *The Vitruvian Square* as a giant, palatial, single-story building. This palace has nine separate rooms – each with distinct walls (although some are shared with a neighbor) and doors that are placed so that each room connects with its neighbors.

Each room of the palace is inhabited by a person or object. Use the charts given earlier in this book to create the residents of your palace.

Now, walk up to one of the rooms and see a closed door. Square 1 would be a good starting place. Notice that the door for that particular room has symbols, colors, shapes, and perhaps words that are particular to the associations for the number you are visiting. Take a moment and focus your intent on visiting this one – this only – room and your desire to learn the lessons and wisdom that are to be found within. Make a note of anything that might be said to you or additional images shown to you as you approach and enter through the door.

Once inside the room, you are greeted by the denizen of that room. Interact with this thing or person. Pay attention to what is happening in the room, itself. What colors do you notice? What sounds do you hear? Has anyone entered the room with you? Does the thing or person that lives in the room have some important message to share with you? Do you have a message for the thing or person in the room? Are you given a gift to take with you when you leave the room?

You will repeat this exploration with each room of *The Vitruvian Palace* – your own investigation of the symbols and people and things that you meet. In this way, *The Vitruvian Square* becomes an intensely personal, fulfilling and lively tool for you. Indeed, this is quite similar to Jung's technique called "Active Imagination."

I suggest working your way through *The Vitruvian Palace* in numerical order. In other words, you will start with Room 1 and work your way up through and including Room 9. When you have finished the initial nine rooms, you can then concentrate on 0 – essentially the attic or high point of the Palace.

As you end your time in a particular room, be certain to thank the people or things you have found within. Thank them for their time. Thank them for their lessons. Thank them for their wisdom. You may then leave through the same door you entered or choose a new door that opens to the next room. Once you leave through a particular door, turn back and visualize the door closing and a large "X" being written across it. This will bring closure, so to speak, to that particular imaginary journey.

I do not recommend working on more than one room at a time nor visiting more than one room per session. You can always pick up where you left off.

PART TWENTY-ONE
THE VITRUVIAN LABYRINTH

The Labyrinth mirrors the wanderings and travails of the hero

in search for meaning and resolution to the vicissitudes of life.

– David Danow (*Models of Narrative: Theory and Practice*)

In Part Twenty I included a discussion on the pathworking and guided imagery techniques that are possible with *The Vitruvian Square* matrix. You'll recall that this entails using your imagination and walking through each of the Places of Power (rooms, so to speak) that make up *The Vitruvian Palace*. In this chapter, we're going to deepen this concept and I am truly excited to share with you the next generation in guided imagery

that is available with *The Vitruvian Square – The Vitruvian Labyrinth!*

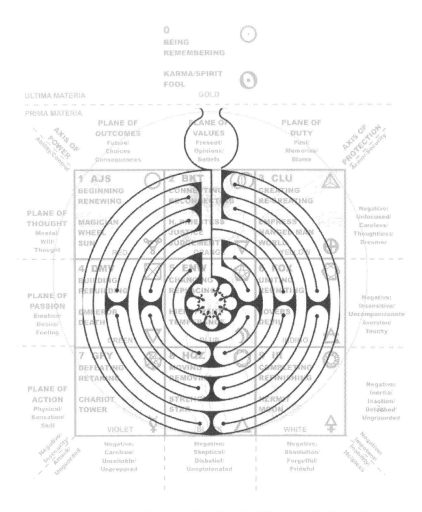

Figure 61 - Vitruvian Square Overlay for Vitruvian Labyrinth

Figure 61 is the fundamental depiction of *The Vitruvian Labyrinth*. This basic version is all you need to take yourself on an incredible inner journey.

A Beginning

Many times, the term "labyrinth" is used interchangeably and confused with the term "maze." A labyrinth is a specific single, non-branching pattern that only leads into the center and back out again. A maze, on the other hand, can be a very complex construction that is a puzzle with choices to be made about the directions to go and the paths to take. There are dead-ends and false starts to a maze, while those don't exist within a true labyrinth.

There are many possible reasons that labyrinths have been created over the ages. Your personal *Vitruvian Labyrinth* is about self-discovery, reawakening, and an individual renaissance. *The Vitruvian Labyrinth*, then, should be thought of as filled to the brim with symbolism and a classical way to walk between the worlds. It is something that is, at once, both your sacred place of power and an inviolate place of reflection. But be warned and excited. Similar to what Yoda said to Luke Skywalker in *The Empire Strikes Back,* what you take into *The Vitruvian Labyrinth*, you will find.

Vitruvian Labyrinth Construction

The Vitruvian Labyrinth gets its inspiration from one of the most famous labyrinths in the world – The 13th century Chartres Labyrinth at the Chartres Cathedral in France. However, *The Vitruvian Labyrinth* was designed specifically for use with *The Vitruvian Square* and so has some special characteristics and symbolism. Here is the basic *Vitruvian Labyrinth*.

Figure 62 - Basic Vitruvian Labyrinth

While *The Vitruvian Labyrinth* certainly has a power on its own, its real energy is experienced when it is used in conjunction with the underlying *Vitruvian Square* approach of a unified divination theory. To assist you in understanding this, our next diagram (Figure 63) is the basic 3×3 magic square pattern of *The Vitruvian Square* overlaid onto *The Vitruvian Labyrinth* so you can see the interplay between the Places of Power, the associated numbers 0 through 9, and the grids.

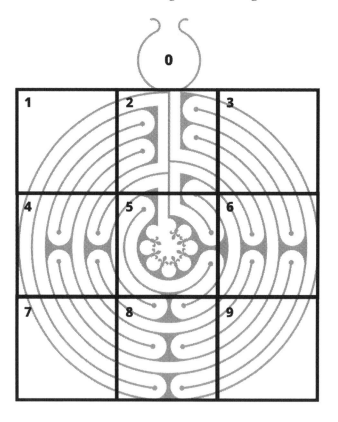

Figure 63 - Vitruvian Labyrinth with Vitruvian Matrix Outline

At the heart of *The Vitruvian Labyrinth* (literally and figuratively) is the construct that our pathway takes us from the heavens and down into a twisting and turning journey of realization and change. We start in Place of Power 0 and then make our way ultimately to the center at Place of Power 5, only to return again – transformed and emboldened – back to the starting point. *The Vitruvian Labyrinth* leads you through a true Hero's Journey when you contemplate the various *Vitruvian Square* associations that the labyrinth takes you through as you "walk" it.

Some Basic Vitruvian Labyrinth Attributes

The Vitruvian Labyrinth is another way of expressing the marriage of heaven and earth (as represented by the square and circle geometry found within Leonardo's The Vitruvian Man). The circle is, at once, a representation of the heavens and the cycle of time, while also being associated with the concepts of initiation, the universe, everything, and completion. The square is a symbol of the earth and our foundation.

The Vitruvian Labyrinth, then, is another way of expressing order, structure, building, and manifestation.

Our labyrinth contains ten circuits (nine outer tracks and the center circle) with only one way in and only one way out (Figure 64).

Each of the ten circuits represents a Place of Power in their own right within *The Vitruvian Square*. Each of these ten circuits corresponds to a different realm (and, indeed, may even be associated with a similar spiritual concept from Buddhism, if you'd like).

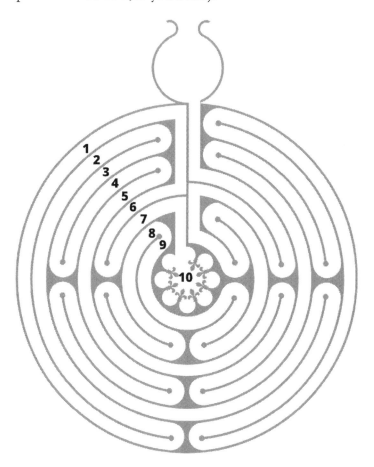

Figure 64 - Vitruvian Labyrinth Circuits

As you will see in the following diagram (Figure 65), *The Vitruvian Labyrinth* can also be divided into four quarters.

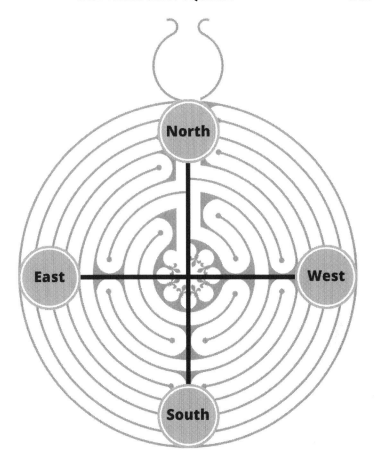

Figure 65 - Vitruvian Labyrinth Cardinal Points

I have discussed many times the various associations for the four cardinal points in various cultures. Among others, you might consider the following correspondences in using the labyrinth:

NORTH = Pentacles = Earth = Winter = Sensation

WEST = Cups = Water = Fall = Feeling

SOUTH = Wands = Fire = Summer = Intuition

EAST = Swords = Air = Spring = Thinking

You will note that, in Figure 65, West is on your right as you look down on the diagram from the outside, while East is on your left. Please remember though that, in working with *The Vitruvian Square*, you are not looking at *The Vitruvian Square* from the outside but as if you were in the matrix looking out. You are putting yourself into the structure and so you are seeing with those eyes. In other words, pretend you are the Vitruvian Man looking out from the matrix and back at yourself. From this position, East is on your right and West is on your left. What might look like an inadvertent reversal, on first blush, is really a deeper layer to working with both the matrix and the labyrinth. You are inside both of them – not merely an observer! (By the way, this also explains why Place of Power 6 is on right as you look down on the matrix and Place of Power 4 is on the left.)

The Vitruvian Labyrinth also contains twenty-two switchbacks or hairpin curves (Figure 66). The number twenty-two is considered a potent and compelling number. It has been described as the number that can turn dreams into reality. It also symbolizes accuracy and balance.

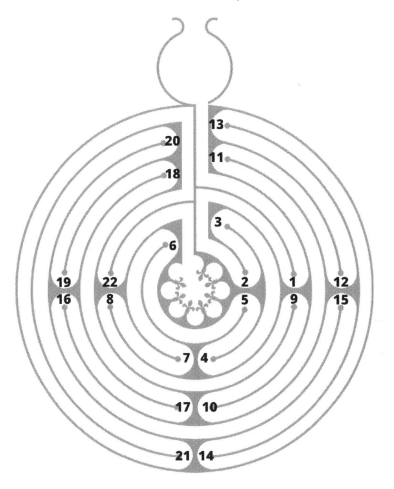

Figure 66 - Vitruvian Labyrinth Hairpin Curves

In addition to the switchbacks, *The Vitruvian Labyrinth* contains six turns (Figure 67).

Figure 67 - Vitruvian Labyrinth Turns

In numerology, the number 6 can mean enlightenment – a lighting of our way – and the expressive nature of the soul. This is the number of truth, love, and balance. It should come as no surprise, then, that the turns of the labyrinth were present at the very beginning and very end of our journey into and out of the labyrinth.

Ten Life Paths

As we have previously seen in Figure 64, there are ten paths (nine concentric tracks and one center circle) that make up *The Vitruvian Labyrinth*. Let's expand on that characteristic a little more. These ten paths represent the inevitable spiritual/mental/psychological journey from life to death and then rebirth; the dynamics that arise from a mixing of both the spiritual and living worlds.

These ten paths are also reflections of the ten Sephirot of Nothingness that make up the Kabbalistic Tree of Life. These paths, then, are to be viewed as the ten different ways that Life manifests itself to you. (You will recall that there are also the twenty-two hairpin curves/switchbacks that relate to the twenty-two letters of the Hebrew alphabet and, in turn, to the twenty-two connectors of The Tree of Life.) When you combine the ten paths with the twenty-two hairpin turns you have thirty-two Paths of Wisdom or acts of creation.

The number 10, by the way, stands for harmony and of the creator entering their creation. It embodies the concept of something being made out of chaos. And it has been called the full course of life.

Here then you have a direct representation of the ten stages of your becoming.

Nine Mystical Spheres

The center of *The Vitruvian Labyrinth* is composed of nine mystical spheres or stations (eight external stations and the one central station around which the eight others revolve); these nine spheres also represent the nine Places of Power of *The Vitruvian Square*. In fact, if you look at the center of the labyrinth, you will see the nine spheres are actually arranged in a 3×3 grid and so the attributes of *The Vitruvian Square's* Place of Power are easily applied.

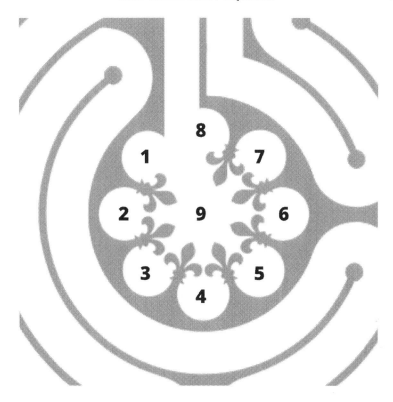

Figure 68 - The Nine Spheres of The Vitruvian Labyrinth

The number 9 is not only the symbol of inspiration, it is a representation of your humanness, itself. As an example, the average pregnancy is nine months. When you reach the center of *The Vitruvian Labyrinth*, you have reached the place of peace where you are born again.

Eight Labryses

There are eight double-headed axes (Labryses) within *The Vitruvian Labyrinth*:

Figure 69 - The Eight Labryses of The Vitruvian Labyrinth

These symbols can be interpreted as both male and female

energies; depending on what you are seeking to find within the labyrinth.

As a symbol of male energy, the double-headed axe can be the equivalent

of a thunderbolt; a very sudden and very effective transfer of energy

from the sky to the ground. As a symbol of female energy, the double-

headed axe is one of ceremony and rebirth.

The number 8 is all about resolution, strong-mindedness, and willpower; an ideal number to represent the Labryses.

Seven Fleurs-di-lis

The center of *The Vitruvian Labyrinth*, on first glance, looks like a circle of thorns; the thorn being a symbol of both obstacles and protection. On closer inspection of the center of the labyrinth, though, you will see that the center design is actually made up of seven fleurs-di-lis; a symbol of The Ideal, life, and light.

Figure 70 - The Seven Fleurs-di-lis of The Vitruvian Labyrinth

The number 7, of course, has a magical and spiritual significance – standing for completion, perfection, and the heavens manifested on earth. The seven fleurs-di-lis remain a mystery to the uninitiated.

First to the Left

When traveling into *The Vitruvian Labyrinth*, you find yourself entering the network of paths just left of center. You then travel all of the inner circuits on the left before completing the inner circuits on the right. From there you are taken to the left outer circuits before being taken to the right outer circuits.

When you are traveling left of center, you are making a symbolic statement of going against the grain, being a rebel, and cementing in place that you are a freethinker. Walking in this manner embodies the fact that you are innovative and certainly not content with things the way they are.

Now, let's start touring how to use our well-built *Vitruvian Labyrinth* path for giving readings. Here are some incredibly simple but potent techniques for you to begin playing with:

A "Figure of Speech" Reading

The Vitruvian Labyrinth is, if nothing else, a representation of our travel through life. Yet, it is something more – it is also about our experience of life. It is a visual provocation for all that we associate with where we are at any given moment. You can quickly see that one of the most all-embracing readings you can give someone – including yourself – is to examine initial, gut reactions to *The Vitruvian Labyrinth*. Follow these steps and you will get an on-the-spot grasp of where a person believes they are right now and how they view their life.

STEP 1: Place *The Vitruvian Labyrinth* diagram (you will find one at the end of the book) in front of your participant with the entrance to the path facing them. To help you visualize the orientation, Place of Power 0 from *The Vitruvian Square* would be closest to your participant and the bottom row of numbers (7, 8, 9) would be closest to you (presuming you are sitting opposite your participant).

STEP 2: Have your participant take a moment and stare at *The Vitruvian Labyrinth*.

STEP 3: Ask your participant to use their imagination and describe what they see before them using three adjectives. Don't explain anything more to the participant. You are seeking their raw reactions to what they are viewing and experiencing.

STEP 4: Use the adjectives you are given to understand the participant's current view of their life situation. While the participant has provided you with adjectives to describe what *The Vitruvian Labyrinth* is like, you will use those same adjectives (or words like those adjectives) to describe what life is for your participant.

The "Moments of Truth" Reading

This is the most expansive and wide-ranging of the readings I will provide to you and is designed to predict and analyze each of the twenty-two major turning points in a person's life. It can be done with just the twenty-two Major Arcana (if you prefer to keep the discussion focused on those archetypes), a full deck of Tarot cards, *The Deck of Shadows*, or any other oracular device that has at least twenty-two items at hand.

Before we delve into this rather lengthy and deep layout, remember that *The Vitruvian Labyrinth* contains twenty-two hairpin turns/switchbacks that represent the transformations or turning points in one's life (Figure 71). These twists/turns/bends/changes occur in a progressive pattern. There are four hairpin bends in the path in the area of the North, five hairpin bends in the area of the West, six hairpin bends in the area of the South, and seven hairpin bends in the area of the East.

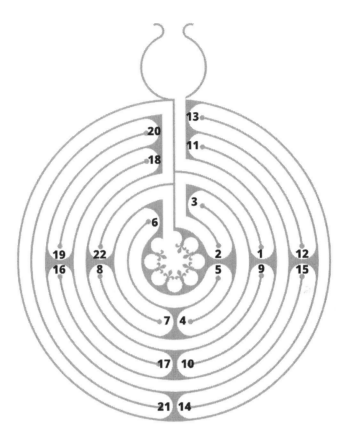

Figure 71 - Vitruvian Labyrinth Hairpin Turns

In this next card layout, we will use Figure 71 as our model.

The major Moments of Truth in one's life can be summarized as occurring in four aspects of life; namely, Faith, Dreams, Desire, and Touch. Those four aspects, in turn, correspond to the four directions we discussed earlier. Those translate, as follows:

FAITH = EAST

DREAMS = SOUTH

DESIRE = WEST

TOUCH = NORTH

This occurs because you can manifest anything with sufficient faith, sufficient dreams, sufficient desire, and a sufficient connection with life. Any suffering you experience is fundamentally caused by a forgetting of your intensity of at least one of those elements.

You only have to understand and use the foregoing essential components (Faith, Dreams, Desire, and Touch) to "read" this spread. Here are the four essential components in more detail:

FAITH – This is what you are convinced by, think of as true, and puzzle over. It is your complete belief and self-confidence in yourself, someone, or something. This is your courage, your bravery, and your optimism. When you lose faith, you no longer trust in yourself or others, and your hopefulness turns to hopelessness. KEYWORDS INCLUDE: faith, trust, believe, confidence, think, determine, judge, consider.

DREAMS – This is what burns inside you, lights you up, and sets your aspirations on fire. It is your ambition, your sense of purpose, and your fantasies. This is what you refuse to live without because it inspires you and helps you to plan for action in the real world. When you lose dreams, you become discouraged, demoralized, and you are prevented from experimenting with new ideas and plans. KEYWORDS INCLUDE: dream, expect, imagine, pretend, assume, presume, consume, roused.

DESIRE – This is your gut feelings, your instincts, and your heartstrings. It is your passion, your love, and your impulses. This is what you want and wish for, and where you admit what you are attracted to. Lose desire, and you lose your wishes for people, things, and events; your want for more in life vanishes. KEYWORDS INCLUDE: desire, passion, love, wish, hope, want, lust, urge.

TOUCH – This is when you grasp something, seize the day, and connect with or reach out to someone. It is your ability to handle anyone or anything. It is your capability for doing things well. It is being in command of your world. When you lose touch, you don't feel that you are competent to apply yourself as you once did. KEYWORDS INCLUDE: touch, grasp, hold, seize, possess, embrace, connect, contain.

Clearly, you can see how, if you lose any of these, you have plainly lost your way on your path of adventure!

Likewise, your bliss easily happens and you experience true pleasure when all of these incredible ingredients are fluidly working in cooperation with each other. The quality of your delight is equal to the quality of how well all of these elements join forces and soar within you.

It is also useful for you to recognize that each of these elements has an association with the four directions I detailed earlier in the book (North, East, South, West) and the suits of the Minor Arcana (Pentacles, Swords, Wands, Cups), as follows:

FAITH = EAST = SWORDS (thinking)

DREAMS = SOUTH = WANDS (intuition)

DESIRE = WEST = CUPS (feeling)

TOUCH = NORTH = PENTACLES (sensation)

Now, on to the layout, itself. It uses twenty-two cards.

STEP 1: Have your deck mixed and cut.

STEP 2: Deal four cards face-down and farthest away from you and closest to your participant (if you are using *The Vitruvian Square*, the matrix design will have Place of Power 0 closest to the participant and Places of Power 7, 8, and 9 closest to you).

STEP 3: Deal five cards face-down and put them to your left.

STEP 4: Deal six cards face-down and place them closest to you.

STEP 5: Finally, deal seven cards face-down to your right.

[RECAP: Your cards should look similar to Figure 72. Don't worry about placing the groups of cards in the exact configuration shown nor do you have to adhere to the precise numerical sequence in the Figure 71. Instead, you will simply place the cards in four, five, six, and seven card groupings that generally coincide with Figure 71.]

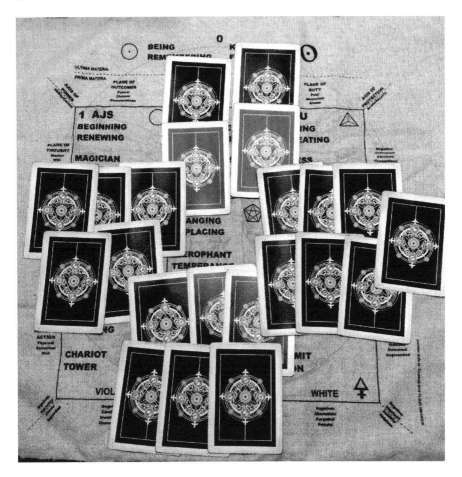

Figure 72 - Moments of Truth Reading with The Deck of Shadows

STEP 6: Have your participant look over the cards and ask them to hand you a card. Whichever card they decide upon is where they are starting within *The Vitruvian Labyrinth*. There is no right or wrong choice here. Rather, just take note of where they are beginning their journey from within the labyrinth (Faith/East/Swords/Thinking, Dreams/South/Wands/Intuition, Desire/West/Cups/Feeling, or Touch/North/Pentacles). Take the card they have selected as their starting point, turn it face-up, and place it to your left and closest to you (below the layout).

STEP 7: Repeat Step 3 with each of the remaining twenty-one cards; each chosen card is turned face-up in turn and placed sequentially to the right of the card chosen before it. Be mindful of how your participant chooses their cards and the locations within the labyrinth from which they come. Note any pattern that emerges in the selection process. Also, pay attention to how they make their choices. Are they hesitant? Excited? Quick? Plodding? For example, are they focused on only one group of cards in a specific location or do they seem to be choosing haphazardly? Are they choosing cards in a circular arrangement or are they choosing cards that are positioned opposite of each other? These observations can all add to your reading.

STEP 8: Look over the twenty-two cards and, beginning with the card that was selected first, let the cards tell the story of your participant's journey through life. Bring all of the things you have noticed about the manner in which the cards were chosen and any selection patterns you observed into the story. Let your heart and your gut drive the story that unfolds for you. Push what your logical mind might otherwise be telling you aside. In other words, just go with the flow of what you see before you.

The "Secret Path" Reading

This is a quick three-card reading that provides you tremendous insight into your participant and clearly tells them where they've just come from, where they are, and where they are going in the near future. It is built around the entrance to the labyrinth, the center of the labyrinth, and a point along the labyrinth's path that has special meaning to your participant.

STEP 1: Have the cards shuffled and mixed.

STEP 2: Select a card and place it face-down closest to your participant. This is where they entered their personal labyrinth and represents where they have just come from.

STEP 3: Select another card and hand it face-down to your participant. Ask them: "Where are you now?" Have them place the card face-down on the table in front of them. Take note of where the card is placed and its relation to where the labyrinth would be if it was actually drawn on the table.

STEP 4: Select a third card and place it face-down in the very center of the table. This is where your participant is going.

STEP 5: Turn the cards over and read them in relation to their positions and meanings.

"The Way In and The Way Out" Reading

Let's explore one last spread you might consider using; something I call "The Way In and The Way Out". The spread uses only six cards and is based solely on the six turns that get you into the labyrinth initially and bring you closest to the center (and back out, again) (Figure 73).

Figure 73 - Vitruvian Labyrinth Turns

STEP 1: Shuffle and mix the cards.

STEP 2: Lay out three cards face-down as shown in Figure 73, above, at positions 1, 2, and 3. These will be placed to your right and to your participant's left. Card 1 is placed closest to your participant. Card 3 is placed closest to you.

STEP 3: Lay out three more cards face-down as shown in Figure 73 in positions 4, 5, and 6. These will be placed to your left and to your participant's right. Card 4 is placed closest to your participant. Card 6 is placed closest to you.

STEP 4: Turn over cards 1, 2, and 3. These represent what your participant brought with them that got them to where they are today. These cards make up the story of the path your spectator took to get into their current situation.

STEP 5: Turn over cards 4, 5, and 6. These represent what your participant is about to learn that will lead them out of or away from their current situation.

Finally, we travel there and back again. As we conclude, we will go on a mighty quest. We are leaving behind the philosophical and abstract discussions and getting down-to-earth – so to speak – about *The Vitruvian Labyrinth*; one of those mysterious elements that lives within *The Vitruvian Square*. As a reminder before we start out on our journey, revisit Figure 61 or the image at the back of the book so you can see *The Vitruvian Labyrinth* overlaid onto *The Vitruvian Square*.

You are going to go on an actual journey along or through this very labyrinth. This is essentially a combination of both a waking dream and deep mediation. Don't over-analyze this before you take your first journey – there will plenty of time for you analytical types to deconstruct the technique after you experience its full effect.

STEP ONE: Open the book to Figure 61 so that *The Vitruvian Labyrinth* is in front of you with the small antechamber at the top (the "0" should be at the top). Take a moment and just look over the entire labyrinth design. In doing so, know that there are five memorable stages to your imminent *Vitruvian Labyrinth* journey:

STAGE 1: The Place Before – This is the obligatory antechamber or entryway into the labyrinth. It is where you will take a moment to deliberately reflect on the reason for your visit upon the path.

STAGE 2: The Quest – This is the serpentine, ten circuit path with its twenty-two turning points that you take to reach the center of the labyrinth.

STAGE 3: The Center of Peace – The promising center and refreshing heart of the labyrinth.

STAGE 4: The Return – The now-worldly-wise path you take back out of the labyrinth.

STAGE 5: The Place After – The same antechamber through which you entered, but now it takes on a new role – a room of gratefulness and reflection.

STEP TWO: Place the forefinger of your non-dominant hand inside the antechamber. Just pause here for a moment, imagining yourself about to embark on an exciting exploit. This is the time when you ask yourself why? – Why are you are starting out on this journey in the first place? What do you hope to find? What do you want to explore? What emotion do you want to confront? Perhaps you want to consider whether you just desire to leave the real world behind for a short time or whether you want to come face-to-face with some fiendish thought that has been plaguing you. The enchanting characteristic of labyrinth work is that it is so personal. There are no wrong reasons for walking a labyrinth. Know only this: to sound like Yoda, again, "you will find only what you bring in!" Now, use your waking imagination and pretend you are standing inside the antechamber, itself. Is it a room? Is it a cave? Are you in a garden or a park? Wherever you imagine yourself to be, bring your creative, inner vision into focus and note as much detail as possible about your surroundings.

STEP THREE: After a short time, you find that a chaperone or guide appears to you in the antechamber. This can be a person, an animal, a fictitious character, anything or anyone. Just let the guide appear to you and start to lead you out of the antechamber and along the path. Move your finger down from the antechamber along the first straight portion of the pathway and towards yourself knowing that your guide is actually leading the way and keeping you shielded. You have started your journey! Pay attention to how you feel as you make your way along the path. Is your path actually a tunnel or are you on a garden pathway? Are there walls or are you on an open trail? Are you descending down into the earth or is the path level and serene? Is the sun shining down on you or do you see the moon or, perhaps, there's no light at all. Notice your emotions. Notice the sounds around you. Notice where you start to linger or perhaps lose your way. Notice the focus it takes to stay on the path with your finger. And . . . notice what your guide is doing or saying as it leads you. All of your sensations and thoughts and feelings are important as they serve as both messages and metaphors for what you are supposed to find inside the labyrinth.

STEP FOUR: As you and your guide come to the end of the straightaway, you make a sharp left turn with your finger. Continue on the path a short distance and you will reach the beginning of your first hairpin curve. Before you actually move into the curve, your guide turns to you and bids you to continue on without it. Thank your guide for traveling with you this far and know that it will be waiting for you at this very spot to lead you back out of the labyrinth when you return.

STEP FIVE: Leaving your guide behind, you move through the first hairpin curve. Continue along the winding path – again, paying attention to how you are feeling, your reactions to the journey, and where your mind is focused.

STEP SIX: Eventually, in your own time and at your own pace, you will arrive at the bosom of *The Vitruvian Labyrinth*. Describe what you see, feel, hear, and experience. Where is this place that you have finally arrived at? When you are ready, place the palm of your non-dominant hand on top of the paper with the center of your palm over the center of the labyrinth. Then repeat to yourself the following incantation: at the center of all peace I stand and naught can harm me here. Now just let feelings of peacefulness and tranquility play with your mind. And as you stray and drift with your own thoughts and your own stillness, you start to notice that a wise thing has become visible in the center of the labyrinth with you. Who or what is this wise thing? And now you learn that you get to ask your wise thing any question at all – something that is important at the moment for you to know or learn. Ask your question of the wise thing and then listen intently for the answer. After you receive the message, thank your wise thing for sharing its knowledge and time with you. And then watch the wise thing slowly fade away.

STEP SEVEN: Stay where you are, with your palm on the paper, for as long as you'd like and enjoy the repose while you muse over the import of the message you were given.

STEP EIGHT: When you are ready, put the forefinger of your non-dominant hand back in the heart of the labyrinth and commence tracing your journey back out of labyrinth the same way that you came in.

STEP NINE: In due course, your finger will return to the place where you left your guide. The guide, of course, is still there, waiting patiently and obediently and expectantly for you. Bid it hello, again, and – tracing the path with your finger – follow it back out towards the antechamber. At the entrance into the antechamber, your guide now signals you goodbye as you trace your finger that final trek into the room from which you started. Take a moment before lifting your finger from the paper to give thanks for what you have experienced and any lessons or messages you have been gifted.

STEP TEN: Take the time needed to think back on what you experienced in the labyrinth, what you were told, what you saw with your inner vision, and what special messages or meanings these have for you. This is a very personal journey you have been on and you are the best person to interpret what you have been gifted along the way.

The use of *The Vitruvian Labyrinth* can be a soulful and passionate daily practice that will bring you comfort and meaning. I must emphasize that there is no one way to walk the labyrinth and, in fact, your journey may be different each time. I want you to remember this. Sometimes, you may move through the path quickly. Other times, you may feel like you're plodding your way along the path. Sometimes, it will feel like magic has happened inside the labyrinth. Other times, it will just be a restful break from the stress of life. Whatever is happening at any given time is precisely where you are supposed to be and what you have to do and it is perfect for you. The important thing is to notice what you are experiencing and remember the feelings, thoughts, messages, etc. that are given to as you complete your journey.

The Vitruvian Labyrinth will provide you with metaphors and messages that should be turned over in your mind immediately after finishing your return out of the antechamber. Write down the inklings, random thoughts, direct messages, and experiences you noticed while walking the path. All of these have significance for you and have a deep-seated message to digest.

PART TWENTY-TWO
THE "I AM PEACE" HO'OPONOPONO PRAYER

You can't forgive without loving.

And I don't mean sentimentality.

I don't mean mush. I mean having enough

courage to stand up and say,

"I forgive. I'm finished with it."

- Maya Angelou

The term "Ho'oponopono", according to Wikipedia, is defined as:

(a) "To put to rights; to put in order or shape, correct, revise, adjust, amend, regulate, arrange, rectify, tidy up make orderly or neat, administer, superintend, supervise, manage, edit, work carefully or neatly; to make ready, as canoemen preparing to catch a wave."

(b) "Mental cleansing: family conferences in which relationships were set right (ho'oponopono) through prayer, discussion, confession, repentance, and mutual restitution and forgiveness."

While there are many claimed authorities on the history of the Ho'Oponopono practice, I think most will agree that Morrnah Nalamaku Simeona, with her adaptation of prayers and rituals, brought Ho'Oponopono into modern times. She taught her version of the Ho'Oponopono practice to, among others, Dr. Ihaleakala Hew Len who revised and refined the process further. He, in turn, taught instructor Mabel Katz and, more famously, Dr. Joe Vitale. Dr. Vitale, in cooperation with Dr. Len (who has now retired), authored the amazing books, Zero Limits: The Secret Hawaiian System for Wealth, Health, Peace, and More, At Zero: The Final Secrets to "Zero Limits" The Quest for Miracles Through Ho'oponopono. Dr. Vitale also offers online Ho'oponopono training and certification.

Morrnah Simeona's version of the Ho'oponopono prayer contained a dozen "steps", breathing protocols, and prayers. Dr. Len streamlined the process into four sentences. Dr. Vitale eventually added one more powerful affirmation to Dr. Len's process. Others, of course, have added their own unique perspectives and techniques along the way.

I invite you to connect with Dr. Vitale and learn more from him regarding Ho'oponopono. In the meantime, I offer you my version of Ho'oponopono and how it plays so wonderfully well with *The Vitruvian Square* and each of the Places of Power.

At its core, Ho'oponopono is about clearing, cleaning, and restoring . . . you. It is purposefully designed to bring you to a place of peace, calm, ease, and bliss. It is a map that can be easily followed to manifest a state of mind and uplifting of the spirit. This, in turn, helps manifest desired or needed outcomes about any issue that is troubling you.

Using a technique similar to what I discussed in Part Nineteen, it is possible to take *The Vitruvian Square* and, in meditating upon each Place of Power (Figure 74), expand upon the Ho'oponopono construct and arrive at ten potent and magical statements:

I am peace.

I am the light.

I am enough.

I am sorry.

I am here.

Please forgive me.

I love you.

Thank you.

I remember who I am.

It is done.

Each statement is intended to be read in order.

0

**I AM
PEACE**

1 **I AM THE LIGHT**	2 **I AM ENOUGH**	3 **I AM SORRY**
4 **I AM HERE**	5 **PLEASE FORGIVE ME**	6 **I LOVE YOU**
7 **THANK YOU**	8 **I REMEMBER WHO I AM**	9 **IT IS DONE**

Figure 74 - The "I am Peace" Ho'Oponopono Prayer

You will find that each statement is in complete synchronicity

with *The Vitruvian Square* matrix. Here is the entire "I Am Peace"

Ho'Oponopono Prayer placed over *The Vitruvian Square*.

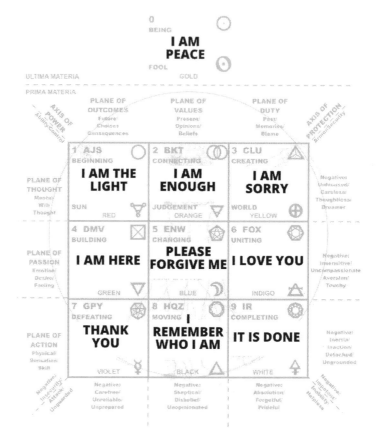

Figure 75 - The "I am Peace" Prayer Vitruvian Square Configuration

You will notice some powerful correspondences.

I am peace. = 0 = The Fool

I am the light. = 1 = The Magician, The Wheel, The Sun

I am enough. = 2 = The High Priestess, Justice, Judgement

I am sorry. = 3 = The Empress, The Hanged Man, The World

I am here. = 4 = The Emperor, Death

Please forgive me. = 5 = The Hierophant, Temperance

I love you. = 6 = The Lovers, The Devil

Thank you. = 7 = The Chariot, The Tower

I remember who I am. = 8 = Strength, The Star

It is done. = 9 = The Hermit, The Moon

All you need do is form some simple and easy-to-remember associations with the 0 through 9 Places of Power and the "I am Peace" Ho'Oponopono Prayer is yours forever to use.

Here are the mnemonics I use with Tarot symbolism:

I am peace. = 0 = Imagine The Fool and the PEACEFUL look on his face.

I am the light. = 1 = Imagine The Magician with the LIGHT of the Sun passing from his upper hand down through his body to the Earth.

I am enough. = 2 = Imagine The High Priestess sitting between her two pillars with just ENOUGH of the scroll in her lap sticking out that you can see it.

I am sorry. = 3 = Imagine The Empress, as a mother figure, saying to a child who is hurt, "I AM SORRY."

I am here. = 4 = Imagine The Emperor confidently sitting on his throne and declaring "I AM HERE."

Please forgive me. = 5 = Imagine The Hierophant taking your confession and you saying, "Father, FORGIVE ME . . ."

I love you. = 6 = Imagine The Lovers saying "I LOVE YOU" to each other.

Thank you. = 7 = Imagine the Charioteer from The Chariot in a victory parade and people yelling out "THANK YOU" to him.

I remember who I am. = 8 = Imagine the female figure in the Strength card REMEBERING that she has the might to overcome the lion.

It is done. = 9 = Imagine The Hermit seeing that his work is DONE and walking away from everything. I like to also use the lyrics from Neil Diamond's song, *DONE Too Soon*, for this, as well.

Here is one way you can put the "I am Peace" Ho'Oponopono Prayer easily and with great consequence to work for you.

STEP 1: Name the issue, thing, or person that is causing you some form of distress or suffering.

STEP 2: Name the distress or suffering you are feeling. Really dig deep and find your most intense emotions.

STEP 3: Name the state of extreme happiness or bliss that you would rather feel, instead.

STEP 4: You can use a version of the well-known Subjective Units of Distress Scale (SUDS) developed by Dr. Joseph Wolpe to now get a baseline of your level of anxiety, fear, stress or tension about a particular situation or person. SUDS is a scale that runs from 0 to 10. The feeling or mood that you identified in Step 3 is 0 and represents being in a place of complete tranquility and ultimate serenity. 10 is that place of you having full-blown anxiety and supreme stress. This is a self-assessment technique where you evaluate how you feel rather than letting someone else tell you how you're feeling.

Take your particular situation or person causing you adversity, hurt, or suffering and ask yourself:

On a scale of 0 to 10 (remember, 0 is utmost calm and happiness and 10 is extreme suffering), what is my level of the feeling I identified in Step 2?

Your answer to this question will be the baseline against which you measure your use of the "I am Peace" Ho'Oponopono Prayer. You want to continue to use the prayer until your stress level moves to 0.

STEP 5: Repeat the "I am Peace" Ho'Oponopono Prayer. Each line has massive significance. Say each word slowly and with purpose. Relish the words. Ask yourself what each sentence means for you.

STEP 6: Only after you say "It is done," do a SUDS check-in with yourself. Whatever level of distress you were feeling, is it lower and closer to 0 now?

STEP 7: Repeat the "I am Peace" Ho'Oponopono Prayer, again, if needed.

During your use of the "I am Peace" Ho'Oponopono Prayer, make sure to notice the thoughts and feelings that you experience. I invite you to journal into them. You'll be surprised at the themes and insights you gain.

Traditionally, Ho'Oponopono is a practice that is done for and on yourself. It is designed to cleanse and clear what is going on in you. You might find, however, that there are times when you want to use the "I am Peace" Ho'Oponopono Prayer on a particular situation or in response to an outside energy. I recommend the following subtle changes to our prayer:

STEP 1: Determine what is causing the consternation or stress or fear in you. Hold that situation or person or outside influence in your thoughts.

STEP 2: Repeat the following:

You are peace.

You are the light.

You are enough.

I am sorry.

I see you.

Please forgive me.

I love you.

Thank you.

I remember who you are.

It is done.

Finally, for those of you with a loving-kindness meditation practice, you can expand on your normal recitations and adapt the "I am Peace" Ho'Oponopono Prayer, as follows:

STEP 1: Find your center. If it helps, repeat the "I am Peace" Ho'Oponopono Prayer for yourself.

STEP 2: Think about the person to whom you want to send loving-kindness. Hold sacred space for this person.

STEP 3: Repeat the following:

May you be at peace.

May you walk in the light.

May you know that you are enough.

May you welcome your mistakes. (or use: I am sorry.)

May you be present.

May you know forgiveness. (or use: Please forgive me.)

May you be loved.

May you be grateful.

May you remember who you are.

It is done.

STEP 4: Bring your attention to your heart center. Take the time you need to bring your intention for loving-kindness to yourself.

Some of you might be asking, by now, "Why am I apologizing?" or "What am I asking forgiveness for?" when you have done nothing wrong. Let's begin with the many studies and concepts that stand for the proposition that the act of forgiveness (whether it's you giving this forgiveness to yourself or you asking for forgiveness from others) is transformative when it comes to your well-being.

There is another aspect to this, as well. Perhaps one of the biggest challenges we all face is the habit we have of separating ourselves from our own divinity and others. This lack of oneness is really what you're apologizing for and for which you are asking forgiveness.

Of course, there's always the line from Dr. Len that speaks volumes: *Have you ever noticed that, whenever there's a problem, you are there?* In other words, the problems and challenges you are experiencing in your life are there because you are going through them. The use of "I am sorry" and "Please forgive me" is a way to quickly address and remove these issues.

CONCLUSION

The Vitruvian Square contains a system and various approaches for readings that I have used for quite some time. To actually reduce these to written form has been a marvelous and profound journey. I will be even more pleased to discover that you have learned and adopted some practical and worthwhile tools, techniques, and information within these pages.

This book is tightly packed with an abundance of insights and knowledge. You don't have to remember everything nor commit it all to memory. Rather, learn the initial format for *The Vitruvian Square*. Once you make sense of the purpose behind the layout of the numbers and associations given, you will be able to easily apply your own intuition and prior reading tools in using *The Vitruvian Square*.

Above all else, have fun with the methods provided so that your use of *The Vitruvian Square* rises to the level of mastery. Both you and the people you read for will be well rewarded.

ACKNOWLEDGMENTS

We are dwarfs astride the shoulders of giants.
We master their wisdom and move beyond it.
Due to their wisdom we grow wise
and are able to say all that we say,
but not because we are greater than they.

\- Isaiah di Trani ben Mali

There are many people to thank and who have contributed to the various versions of this.

My profound thanks to Jerome Finley and Enrique Enriquez for being part of this from the beginning. Jerome is a shamanic healer and reader whose deep insights and encouragement spurred me to release the original book out into the world. Enrique is not only what he terms a "visual thinker," he is a phenomenal poet when it comes to the Tarot and translations. He continues to inspire me with his insights. These two magical beings – people who have graced me with their friendship, with their generosity, and support – made what you are holding possible.

Ed Peterson, the author of "Numerology," was also gracious with his valuable time and reviewed an initial draft of the first edition of this book. He then painstakingly wrote me back, bit by bit, as he made his way through the pages and offered priceless advice and comments.

Needless to say, this book could not have been written without the multitude of people who have received readings, insights, and counseling from me. Each of you has a special place within this book, as well, for the impact you have brought upon my abilities and awareness.

Denise Welch, Erin Halas, and Todd Landman each took time from their otherwise busy lives to read through initial drafts and provide their insights, corrections, and suggestions. Thank you. Thank you. Thank you. Your love is felt more than you know. I trust you feel mine in return.

Anthony Jacquin is one of those rare geniuses who not only thinks genius thoughts, he is able to express them in ways that inspire others and draws people deeper into the fabric of life. I am honored that he chose to write the foreword to this new edition.

Paul Green has given me both moral support and marketing encouragement for decades. He is one of those trusted magical friends who helps guide me and keeps me floating through the sometimes crazy-making world of entertainment. Thank you, Paul, for being such a tremendous friend.

To Dean Montalbano – my publisher for the first edition of this book – thank you for having a vision that supported the adventure this book has taken us on. I am eternally appreciative for all you have done and your encouragement for this new version of the book.

My dear family has permitted me the time and energy to explore other realms. They have given me the luxury and support to trust in the concepts you will be reading. For that, I am truly blessed and grateful.

Finally, my wife, Carolyn, has been a partner, cheerleader, editor, creative advisor, and confidante through each step of the creative process. She has patiently allowed me to have a "writer's life." She has surgically offered recommendations and ideas that she believes you, the reader, would appreciate. Her love has seen me through this journey and kept me inspired and excited. What more could anyone want? Thank you, *a Stóirín, a Grá.*

VITRUVIAN SQUARE CORRESPONDENCES

PLACE OF POWER 0

Meaning: Being, Remembering
Alphabet:
Major Arcana: Fool
Appears on Which Die: 10-Sided
Platonic Solid:
Mythic Reading:
Color: Gold
Astrology: Aquarius
Subconscious:
Of Things Lost:
Palmistry:
Alchemy (I): Gold
Alchemy (II):
Alchemy (III):
Alchemy (IV):
I Ching:
"I am Peace" Prayer: I am peace.

PLACE OF POWER 1

Meaning: Beginning, Renewing
Alphabet: A, J, S
Major Arcana: Magician, Wheel, Sun
Appears on Which Die: 4-Sided, 6-Sided, 8-Sided,
                            10-Sided, 12-Sided, 20-Sided
Platonic Solid: Circle
Mythic Reading: The Call to Adventure
Color: Red
Astrology: Gemini, Virgo, Sagittarius, Leo
Subconscious: "Follow your creativity," "Tell a story,"
                "Be accessible," "Be Happy"
Of Things Lost: Main part of the house, living room,
                    bedroom near white linen
Palmistry: Authority, Teacher's Square

Alchemy (I): Primal Mud
Alchemy (II): Begin
Alchemy (III): Passive
Alchemy (IV): Calcination
I Ching: Water
"I am Peace" Prayer: I am the light.

PLACE OF POWER 2

Meaning: Connecting, Reconnecting
Alphabet: B, K, T
Major Arcana: High Priestess, Justice, Judgement
Appears on Which Die: 4-Sided, 6-Sided, 8-Sided,
                    10-Sided, 12-Sided, 20-Sided
Platonic Solid: Vesica Piscis
Mythic Reading: Refusal of the Call
Color: Orange
Astrology: Moon, Libra, Pluto
Subconscious: "Learn secrets," "Show mercy," "Remember"
Of Things Lost: In the house, In or near a vase or bowl,
                    Someone will help find
Palmistry: Seriousness, Girdle of Venus
Alchemy (I): Earth
Alchemy (II): Cold
Alchemy (III): Passive
Alchemy (IV): Dissolution
I Ching: Earth
"I am Peace" Prayer: I am enough.

PLACE OF POWER 3

Meaning: Creating, Recreating
Alphabet: C, L, U
Major Arcana: Empress, Hanged Man, World
Appears on Which Die: 4-Sided, 6-Sided, 8-Sided,
                    10-Sided, 12-Sided, 20-Sided
Platonic Solid: Triangle
Mythic Reading: Supernatural Aid
Color: Yellow

Astrology: Taurus, Libra, Pisces, Capricorn
Subconscious: "Give comfort and protection,"
                        "Hold to your possessions"
Of Things Lost: In a passage, Between papers, Where men congregate
Palmistry: Communication, Empathy
Alchemy (I): Salt
Alchemy (II): Create
Alchemy (III): Active
Alchemy (IV): Separation
I Ching: Thunder
"I am Peace" Prayer: I am sorry.

PLACE OF POWER 4

Meaning: Building, Rebuilding
Alphabet: D, M, V
Major Arcana: Emperor, Death
Appears on Which Die: 4-Sided, 6-Sided, 8-Sided,
                        10-Sided, 12-Sided, 20-Sided
Platonic Solid: Square
Mythic Reading: Crossing the Threshold
Color: Green
Astrology: Aries, Scorpio
Subconscious: "Pursue your desires," "Be unforgettable," "Karma"
Of Things Lost: The item is not lost, It's not in your possession
Palmistry: Practicality, Willpower
Alchemy (I): Water
Alchemy (II): Wet
Alchemy (III): Passive
Alchemy (IV): Conjunction
I Ching: Wind
"I am Peace" Prayer: I am here.

PLACE OF POWER 5

Meaning: Changing, Replacing
Alphabet: E, N, W
Major Arcana: Hierophant, Temperance
Appears on Which Die: 6-Sided, 8-Sided,

10-Sided, 12-Sided, 20-Sided
Platonic Solid: Pentagon
Mythic Reading: Belly of the Whale
Color: Blue
Astrology: Taurus, Sagittarius
Subconscious: "Know your fears," "Concede," "Seek alchemy"
Of Things Lost: Under/near headwear
                    It will be found when you stop looking
Palmistry: Mystic Cross, St. Andrew's Cross
Alchemy (I): Spirit
Alchemy (II): Preserve
Alchemy (III):
Alchemy (IV): Mortification
I Ching:
"I am Peace" Prayer: Please forgive me.

PLACE OF POWER 6

Meaning: Uniting, Reuniting
Alphabet: F, O, X
Major Arcana: Lovers, Devil
Appears on Which Die: 6-Sided, 8-Sided,
                    10-Sided, 12-Sided, 20-Sided
Platonic Solid: Hexagon
Mythic Reading: Meeting with the Goddess
Color: Indigo
Astrology: Gemini, Capricorn
Subconscious: "Stay loyal to those you love," "Set some voluntary limits"
Of Things Lost: Near footwear, On a shelf or stand
Palmistry: Relationships, Courage
Alchemy (I): Air
Alchemy (II): Dry
Alchemy (III): Active
Alchemy (IV): Fermentation
I Ching: Heaven
"I am Peace" Prayer: I love you.

PLACE OF POWER 7

Meaning: Defeating, Retaking
Alphabet: G, P, Y
Major Arcana: Chariot, Tower
Appears on Which Die: 8-Sided, 10-Sided, 12-Sided, 20-Sided
Platonic Solid: Heptagon
Mythic Reading: The Ultimate Boon
Color: Violet
Astrology: Cancer, Mars
Subconscious: "Use your anger," "Show some self-restraint,"
        "Disruption comes naturally"
Of Things Lost: The item will not be found, Deceit is involved,
        Ask someone
Palmistry: Vitality, Power
Alchemy (I): Quicksilver
Alchemy (II): Destroy
Alchemy (III): Passive
Alchemy (IV): Combustion
I Ching: Lake
"I am Peace" Prayer: Thank you.

PLACE OF POWER 8

Meaning: Moving, Removing
Alphabet: H, Q, Z
Major Arcana: Strength, Star
Appears on Which Die: 8-Sided, 10-Sided, 12-Sided, 20-Sided
Platonic Solid: Octagon
Mythic Reading: Master of the Two Worlds
Color: Black
Astrology: Leo, Aquarius
Subconscious: "Think things over," "Have courage,"
        "Be filled with promise"
Of Things Lost: Found on a shelf or ledge, In a field,
        Connected to illness
Palmistry: Travel, Resistance
Alchemy (I): Fire
Alchemy (II): Hot

Alchemy (III): Active
Alchemy (IV): Distillation
I Ching: Mountain
"I am Peace" Prayer: I remember who I am.

PLACE OF POWER 9

Meaning: Completing, Refinishing
Alphabet: I, R
Major Arcana: Hermit, Moon
Appears on Which Die: 10-sided, 12-sided, 20-sided
Platonic Solid: Nonahedron
Mythic Reading: Freedom to Live
Color: White
Astrology: Virgo, Pisces
Subconscious: "Walk away," "Use the past to help you,"
           "Be filled with wonder"
Of Things Lost: It is with a child, May have been lost in a quarrel
Palmistry: Clairvoyance, Metaphysics
Alchemy (I): Sulphur
Alchemy (II): End
Alchemy (III): Active
Alchemy (IV): Coagulation
I Ching: Fire
"I am Peace" Prayer: It is done.

WORKSHEET

Use the following diagram to create your own

Associations for the Places of Power within The Vitruvian Square.

0
BEING
REMEMBERING

	PLANE OF OUTCOMES	PLANE OF VALUES	PLANE OF DUTY	
AXIS OF POWER / Ability / Control	Future Choices Consequences	Present Opinions Beliefs	Past Memories Blame	AXIS OF PROTECTION / Armor / Security
PLANE OF THOUGHT Mental Will Thought	**1 AJS** BEGINNING RENEWING	**2 BKT** CONNECTING RECONNECTING	**3 CLU** CREATING RECREATING	Negative: Unfocused Careless Thoughtless Dreamer
PLANE OF PASSION Emotion Desire Feeling	**4 DMV** BUILDING REBUILDING	**5 ENW** CHANGING REPLACING	**6 FOX** UNITING REUNITING	Negative: Insensitive Uncompassionate Aversion Touchy
PLANE OF ACTION Physical Sensation Skill	**7 GPY** DEFEATING RETAKING	**8 HQZ** MOVING REMOVING	**9 IR** COMPLETING REFINISHING	Negative: Inertia Inaction Detached Ungrounded
Negative: Insecurity Attack Unguarded	Negative: Carefree Unreliable Unprepared	Negative: Skeptical Disbelief Unopinionated	Negative: Absolution Forgetful Prideful	Negative: Impotent Inability Helpless

WORKSHEET

Use the following diagram to create your own

Associations for the Places of Power within The Vitruvian Square.

0
BEING
REMEMBERING

	PLANE OF OUTCOMES	PLANE OF VALUES	PLANE OF DUTY	
AXIS OF POWER — Ability / Control	Future Choices Consequences	Present Opinions Beliefs	Past Memories Blame	*AXIS OF PROTECTION* — Armor / Security
PLANE OF THOUGHT Mental Will Thought	**1 AJS** BEGINNING RENEWING	**2 BKT** CONNECTING RECONNECTING	**3 CLU** CREATING RECREATING	Negative: Unfocused Careless Thoughtless Dreamer
PLANE OF PASSION Emotion Desire Feeling	**4 DMV** BUILDING REBUILDING	**5 ENW** CHANGING REPLACING	**6 FOX** UNITING REUNITING	Negative: Insensitive Uncompassionate Aversion Touchy
PLANE OF ACTION Physical Sensation Skill	**7 GPY** DEFEATING RETAKING	**8 HQZ** MOVING REMOVING	**9 IR** COMPLETING REFINISHING	Negative: Inertia Inaction Detached Ungrounded
Negative: *Insecurity* *Attack* *Unguarded*	Negative: Carefree Unreliable Unprepared	Negative: Skeptical Disbelief Unopinionated	Negative: Absolution Forgetful Prideful	*Negative:* *Impotent* *Inability* *Helpless*

WORKSHEET

Use the following diagram to create your own

Associations for the Places of Power within The Vitruvian Square.

0
BEING
REMEMBERING

	PLANE OF OUTCOMES Future Choices Consequences	PLANE OF VALUES Present Opinions Beliefs	PLANE OF DUTY Past Memories Blame	
AXIS OF POWER Ability / Control				AXIS OF PROTECTION Armor / Security
PLANE OF THOUGHT Mental Will Thought	**1 AJS** BEGINNING RENEWING	**2 BKT** CONNECTING RECONNECTING	**3 CLU** CREATING RECREATING	Negative: Unfocused Careless Thoughtless Dreamer
PLANE OF PASSION Emotion Desire Feeling	**4 DMV** BUILDING REBUILDING	**5 ENW** CHANGING REPLACING	**6 FOX** UNITING REUNITING	Negative: Insensitive Uncompassionate Aversion Touchy
PLANE OF ACTION Physical Sensation Skill	**7 GPY** DEFEATING RETAKING	**8 HQZ** MOVING REMOVING	**9 IR** COMPLETING REFINISHING	Negative: Inertia Inaction Detached Ungrounded
Negative: Insecurity Attack Unguarded	Negative: Carefree Unreliable Unprepared	Negative: Skeptical Disbelief Unopinionated	Negative: Absolution Forgetful Prideful	Negative: Impotent Inability Helpless

WORKSHEET

Use the following diagram to practice your own
Vitruvian Square divination while reading the book.

0

BEING
REMEMBERING

KARMA/SPIRIT
FOOL

ULTIMA MATERIA   GOLD

PRIMA MATERIA

	PLANE OF OUTCOMES Future Choices Consequences	PLANE OF VALUES Present Opinions Beliefs	PLANE OF DUTY Past Memories Blame	
PLANE OF THOUGHT Mental Will Thought	**1 AJS** BEGINNING RENEWING MAGICIAN WHEEL SUN RED	**2 BKT** CONNECTING RECONNECTING H. PRIESTESS JUSTICE JUDGEMENT ORANGE	**3 CLU** CREATING RECREATING EMPRESS HANGED MAN WORLD YELLOW	Negative: Unfocused Careless Thoughtless Dreamer
PLANE OF PASSION Emotion Desire Feeling	**4 DMV** BUILDING REBUILDING EMPEROR DEATH GREEN	**5 ENW** CHANGING REPLACING HIEROPHANT TEMPERANCE BLUE	**6 FOX** UNITING REUNITING LOVERS DEVIL INDIGO	Negative: Insensitive Uncompassionate Aversion Touchy
PLANE OF ACTION Physical Sensation Skill	**7 GPY** DEFEATING RETAKING CHARIOT TOWER VIOLET	**8 HQZ** MOVING REMOVING STRENGTH STAR BLACK	**9 IR** COMPLETING REFINISHING HERMIT MOON WHITE	Negative: Inertia Inaction Detached Ungrounded

AXIS OF POWER — Ability / Control

AXIS OF PROTECTION — Armor / Security

Negative: Insecurity Attack Unguarded

Negative: Impotent Inability Helpless

Negative: Carefree Unreliable Unprepared	Negative: Skeptical Disbelief Unopinionated	Negative: Absolution Forgetful Prideful

WORKSHEET

Use the following diagram to practice your own
Vitruvian Square divination while reading the book.

0

BEING
REMEMBERING

KARMA/SPIRIT
FOOL

GOLD

ULTIMA MATERIA

PRIMA MATERIA

AXIS OF POWER
Ability / Control

AXIS OF PROTECTION
Armor / Security

	PLANE OF OUTCOMES Future Choices Consequences	PLANE OF VALUES Present Opinions Beliefs	PLANE OF DUTY Past Memories Blame	
PLANE OF THOUGHT Mental Will Thought	**1 AJS** BEGINNING RENEWING MAGICIAN WHEEL SUN RED	**2 BKT** CONNECTING RECONNECTING H. PRIESTESS JUSTICE JUDGEMENT ORANGE	**3 CLU** CREATING RECREATING EMPRESS HANGED MAN WORLD YELLOW	Negative: Unfocused Careless Thoughtless Dreamer
PLANE OF PASSION Emotion Desire Feeling	**4 DMV** BUILDING REBUILDING EMPEROR DEATH GREEN	**5 ENW** CHANGING REPLACING HIEROPHANT TEMPERANCE BLUE	**6 FOX** UNITING REUNITING LOVERS DEVIL INDIGO	Negative: Insensitive Uncompassionate Aversion Touchy
PLANE OF ACTION Physical Sensation Skill	**7 GPY** DEFEATING RETAKING CHARIOT TOWER VIOLET	**8 HQZ** MOVING REMOVING STRENGTH STAR BLACK	**9 IR** COMPLETING REFINISHING HERMIT MOON WHITE	Negative: Inertia Inaction Detached Ungrounded

Negative:
Insecurity
Attack
Unguarded

Negative:
Carefree
Unreliable
Unprepared

Negative:
Skeptical
Disbelief
Unopinionated

Negative:
Absolution
Forgetful
Prideful

Negative:
Impotent
Inability
Helpless

WORKSHEET

Use the following diagram to go on your own Vitruvian Labyrinth Journey.

The "I am Peace" Ho'Oponopono Prayer

I am peace.

I am the light.

I am enough.

I am sorry.

I am here.

Please forgive me.

I love you.

Thank you.

I remember who I am.

It is done.

The "I am Peace" Ho'Oponopono Prayer

(for use with another person)

You are peace.

You are the light.

You are enough.

I am sorry.

I see you.

Please forgive me.

I love you.

Thank you.

I remember who you are.

It is done.

The "I am Peace" Ho'Oponopono Prayer

(the loving-kindness approach)

May you be at peace.

May you walk in the light.

May you know that you are enough.

May you welcome your mistakes. (or use: I am sorry.)

May you be present.

May you know forgiveness. (or use: Please forgive me.)

May you be loved.

May you be grateful.

May you remember who you are.

It is done.

SELECTED BIBLIOGRAPHY AND RESOURCES

About Numerology, <u>Western Chinese Numerology</u>.
<http://www.aboutnumerology.com/westernchinesenumerology.php

De Laurence, L.W., <u>Ancient Divination by the Wheel of Pythagoras</u>.
Chicago, De Laurence, Scott & Co., 1916

Diamond, Kartar, <u>Feng Shui for Skeptics - Real Solutions Without Superstition</u>. Culver City, Four Pillars Publishing, 2004

Enriquez, Enrique, <u>tarology - the game of seeing</u>.
<http://tarology.wordpress.com/>

essortment, <u>Basic Chinese Numerology</u>.
<http://www.essortment.com/all/chinesenumerolo_rehm.htm>

Flornoy, Jean-Claude, <u>The Tarot of Jean Noblet</u>. <http://www.tarot-history.com/Jean-Noblet>

Grossberg, Scott, <u>The Deck of Shadows</u>.
<http://thinkingmagically.com>

Grossberg, Scott, <u>The Masks of Tarot</u>. Orlando, Leaping Lizards Publishing, 2009

Hauck, Dennis William, <u>The Complete Idiot's Guide to Alchemy</u>. New York, Alpha Books, 2008

James, Tadd and Wyatt Woodsmall, <u>Time Line Therapy and the Basis of Personality</u>. Capitola, Meta Publications, 1988

Javane, Faith and Dusty Bunker, <u>Numerology and the Divine Triangle</u>. Atglen, Pennsylvania, Whitford Press, 1971

Jung, CG (translated by R.F.C. Hull), <u>Psychology and Alchemy</u>. New York, Princeton University Press, 1953

Laserquist, Kay and Lisa Lenard, <u>The Complete Idiot's Guide to Numerology</u>. New York, Alpha Books, 2004

SELECTED BIBLIOGRAPHY AND RESOURCES (CONT'D)

Luscher, Max, The Luscher Color Test. New York, Pocket Books, 1969

Moore, Robert and Douglas Gillette, King, Warrior, Magician, Love - Rediscovering the Archetypes of the Mature Masculine. New York, Harper Collins, 1991

Moore, Robert, Structures of Self, <http://www.robertmoore-phd.com/index.cfm?fuseaction=page.display&page_id=32>

Omarr, Sydney, Thought Dial. North Hollywood; Melvin Powers/Wilshire Book Company, 1962

Sepharial (Dr. Walter Gorn Old), The Kabala of Numbers. Philadelphia; David McKay Company, 1920

Templeton, RoseMaree, Numerology - Numbers and Their Influence. Dulwich Hill, Australia, Rockpool Publishing, 2007

Vitale, Joe, At Zero: The Quest for Miracles Through Ho'Oponopono. New Jersey; John Wiley & Sons, 2014

Vitale, Joe and Ihaleakala Hew Len, Zero Limits: The Secret Hawaiian System for Wealth, Health, Peace, and More. New Jersey; John Wiley & Sons, 2007

Webster, Richard, Numerology Magic. Minnesota; Llewellyn Worldwide, 1998

Wolfe, Amber, In the Shadow of the Shaman: Connecting with Self, Nature & Spirit. Minnesota; Llewellyn Publications, 2002

Zimbardo, Philip and John Boyd, The Time Paradox: The New Psychology of Time That Will Change Your Life. New York, Free Press, 2009

A NOTE ON THE AUTHOR

Scott Grossberg's work as a life and business coach, consultant, and instructor honors and interprets a variety of world traditions but finds its foundation in shamanic and mystical processes. He has conducted private training and corporate workshops for more than 40 years and his work highlights the intersection of business and personal growth. Scott is the author of the Amazon bestselling and critically acclaimed books, "The Most Magical Secret - 4 Weeks to an Ecstatic Life," "The Vitruvian Square: A Handbook of Divination Discoveries," "The Masks of Tarot: Betraying the Face of Illusion," "The Million Dollar iPad: Secrets for Increasing Your Profits, Productivity and Business Performance," and "The iPad Lawyer: Real Secrets for Your Business Success." He is a practicing attorney and received his undergraduate degree in Philosophy (with a minor in Theatre Arts). Scott has certifications in life coaching, hypnotherapy, NLP, and Ho'oponopono.

From world-class entertainers to influential political figures to elite companies to business executives to those who are simply "starting out," Scott works with individuals from many different experiences and from all walks of life.

Scott is a member of the National Speakers Association, Association for Comprehensive Energy Psychology, Foundation for Shamanic Studies, Academy of Magical Arts (the Magic Castle in Hollywood), International Brotherhood of Magicians, and British Society of Mystery Performers. He lives in Southern California.

scottgrossberg.com
thinkingmagically.com
facebook.com/scottgrossberg
@sgrossberg